Take-Home Leveled Readers

Below-level

Science

Editorial Offices: Glenview, Illinois • Parsippany, New Jersey • New York, New York
Sales Ofices: Needham, Massachusetts • Duluth, Georgia • Glenview, Illinois
Coppell, Texas • Sacramento, California • Mesa, Arizona

PEARSON
Scott
Foresman

sfsuccessnet.com

ISBN: 0-328-19721-1

2 3 4 5 6 7 8 9 10 V004 13 12 11 10 09 08 07 06 05

Table of Contents

To the Teacher

Scott Foresman provides three Leveled Readers for every chapter of *Scott Foresman Science*, Grades 1–6: a *Below-Level Leveled Reader*, an *On-Level Leveled Reader*, and an *Advanced Leveled Reader*.

All three readers teach the same science concepts, same vocabulary, address the same target reading skill and contain the same graphic organizer as the corresponding student edition chapter, just at three different reading levels—providing access to important science content for all students. The On-level and Advanced readers also use additional examples to enrich the chapter and extend ideas

This book contains reproducible copies of the Below-Level Leveled Readers for Grade 2. These are designed for you to reproduce and send home with your students as appropriate. Encourage students to share these books with parents or family members in order to practice reading skills and reinforce science content.

Online versions of these and other readers are also available through the Scott Foresman Leveled Reader Database.

All About
Plants

by Leslie Ann Rotsky

Genre	Comprehension Skill	Text Features	Science Content
Nonfiction	Predict	• Captions • Labels • Glossary	Plants

Scott Foresman Science 2.1

What did you learn?

1. What are the four parts of a plant?

2. What are two groups of plants?

3. **Writing** in Science In this book you read about ways plants are adapted to their environments. Write to explain two of these ways. Use words from the book as you write.

4. **Predict** What would happen if you put a plant in a very dark room without any windows?

Photographs: Every effort has been made to secure permission and provide appropriate credit for photographic material. The publisher deeply regrets any omission and pledges to correct errors called to its attention in subsequent editions. Unless otherwise acknowledged, all photographs are the property of Scott Foresman, a division of Pearson Education. Photo locators denoted as follows: Top (T), Center (C), Bottom (B), Left (L), Right (R) Background (Bkgd)
Title Page: ©DK Images 3 Corbis 4 (Bkgd, BL) ©DK Images 6 (CC) ©DK Images, (B) ©Michael Boys/ Corbis 7 (T) ©Ted Mead/PhotoLibrary, (CR) ©ChromaZone Images/Index Stock Imagery, (CR) ©DK Images, (B) ©Scott Camazine/Photo Researchers, Inc. 8 (CC) Ted Levin/Animals Animals/Earth Scenes, (R) Steve Kaufman/Corbis 10 (B) ©Bill Ross/Corbis, (TC) ©DK Images 11 (TR) Getty Images, (B) ©Ted Mead/PhotoLibrary 12 (B) ©M.P. Kahl/DRK Photo 13 (R) Royalty-Free/Corbis, (CR) ©DK Images 15 (Bkgd) ©Bob Wickham/PhotoLibrary, (BR, TR) ©DK Images 17 (Bkgd) Getty Images, (TR) ©Pat O'Hara/ Corbis, (BR) ©David Muench/Corbis 19 (TR) Steve Kaufman/Corbis, (BR) Patti Murray/Animals Animals/ Earth Scenes, (Bkgd) Randall Hyman Photography 21 (BR) ©OSF/Animals Animals/Earth Scenes, (TR) Image Quest 3-D/NHPA Limited, (Bkgd) ©David Muench 22 (TR) ©DK Images, (CC) Corbis, (B) Richard Hamilton Smith/Corbis 23 (TR) ©Stephen Dalton/NHPA Limited, (B) David Middleton/NHPA Limited

ISBN: 0-328-13769-3

Glossary

adapted   changed to be able to live in a certain environment

environment   a kind of place with living and nonliving things

flower   the part of a plant that makes seeds or fruit

leaves   flat, green parts growing from the stem of a plant

nutrients   food that living things need to grow

prairie   a place with flat land, a lot of grass, and a few trees

roots   parts of a plant that grows into the ground

stem   the part of a plant that grows up from the ground

All About Plants

by Leslie Ann Rotsky

What are the parts of a plant?

Plants need water, air, and sun.
Plants need space.
Plants need nutrients.
Nutrients are the food that living things
need to grow.
Plants get nutrients from soil and water.

Every plant needs food, water, air, and
sunlight to grow!

Plants are adapted to their environments.
Plants live in many kinds of places.

Plant Parts

Plants have four parts.
The parts are the roots, stem, leaves,
and flowers.
These parts help the plant get what it needs.

Roots grow into the soil.
Roots hold a plant in place.
Roots take water and nutrients from the soil to the stem.

The **stem** takes water and nutrients to the leaves.
The stem holds up the plant.

A sundew plant has hairs that trap insects. The plant gets some nutrients from the insects.

A venus's flytrap also gets some nutrients from insects.

How are some marsh plants adapted?

A marsh is a wet environment.
Many plants grow in a marsh.

The soil in a marsh may not
have many nutrients.
Plants in a marsh get nutrients
in other ways.

Cattails grow in wet
soil. They are adapted
to get nutrients from
water in the soil.

Leaves use sunlight, air, and water to
make food for the plant.

Many plants have flowers.
A **flower** makes seeds.
Seeds make new plants.

How are seeds scattered?

Plants grow from seeds.
When seeds are spread out, they have
room to grow.
Scatter means to spread out.

The fruits of a maple tree
look like wings. This shape
helps them scatter.

The fruits of a
water lily have
seeds. The fruits
float on water.

The saguaro cactus has a
long, thick stem. The stem
holds water.

The octopus tree has short
leaves and long spines.
The spines keep the plant
safe from animals that
want to eat it.

How are some desert plants adapted?

Many deserts are sunny and hot all day.
Deserts can be cool at night.
Deserts get little rain.

Some desert plants are adapted to hold water for a long time.

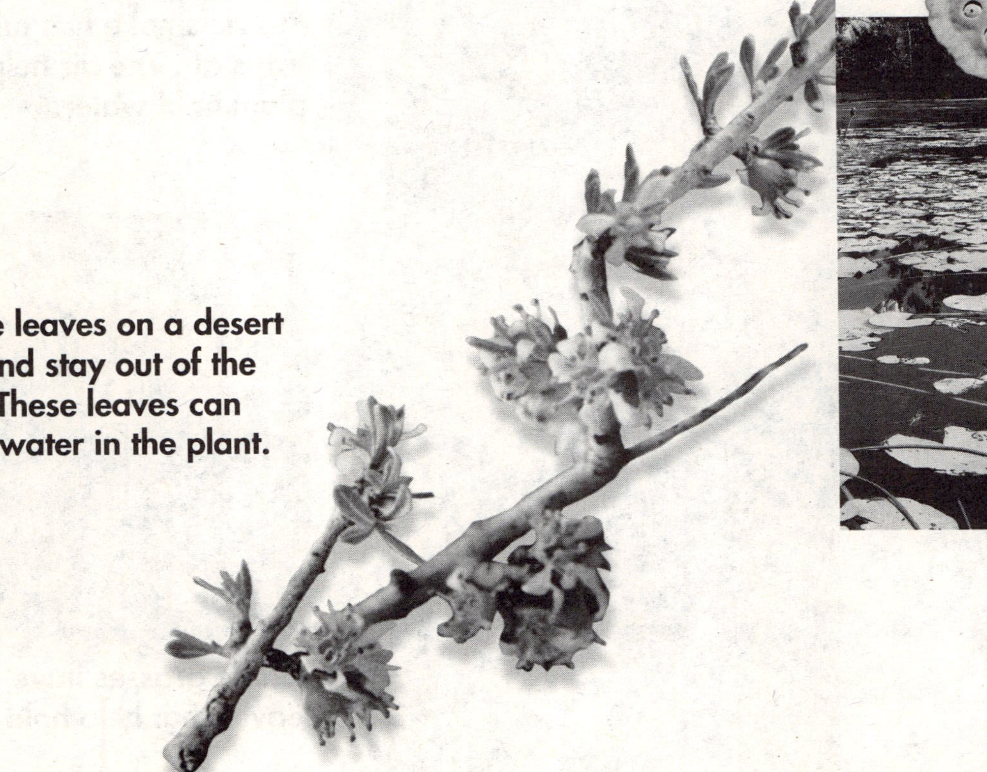

Some leaves on a desert almond stay out of the sun. These leaves can hold water in the plant.

Fruits cover seeds.
Fruits keep seeds safe.
Fruits help scatter seeds.
Some fruits travel by air or water.
Some fruits get stuck on animals.
Animals carry seeds to new places.

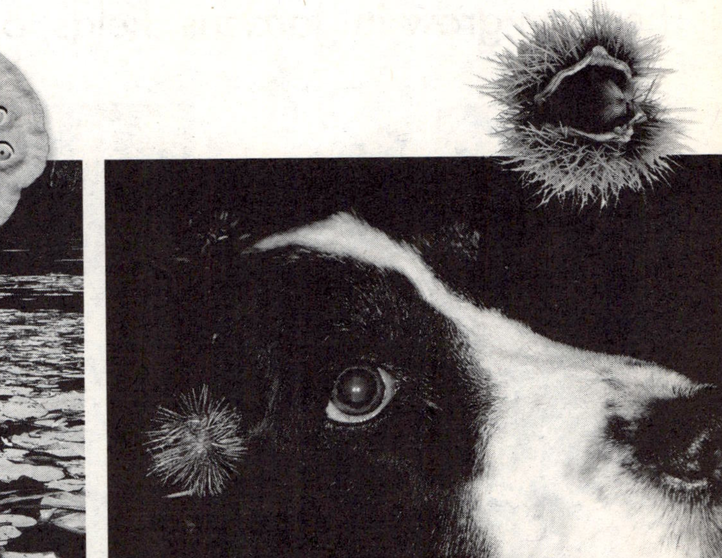

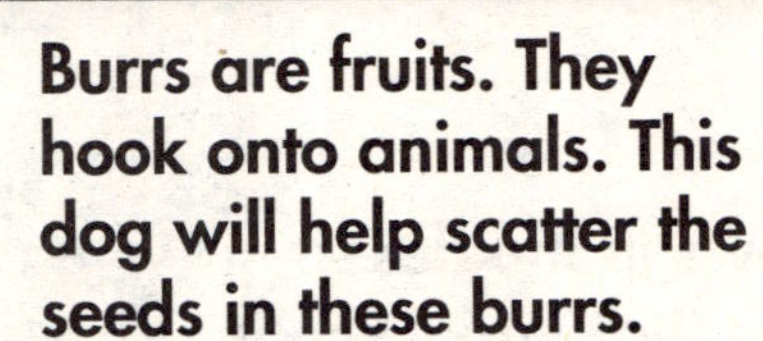

Burrs are fruits. They hook onto animals. This dog will help scatter the seeds in these burrs.

How are plants grouped?

One group of plants has flowers.
The other group of plants does not
have flowers.

Plants with flowers grow in many places.
They can grow in gardens, fields, or deserts.

A cactus grows in the desert.
It has flowers that make seeds.
New cactus plants grow from
the seeds.

Prairie smoke has fuzz that
traps air. The air helps the
plant hold water.

Prairie grasses have small
leaves that help hold water.

How are some prairie plants adapted?

Many plants live in a prairie environment.
A **prairie** has lots of grass and few trees.

Many prairies have hot summers with
little rain.
Some prairie plants are adapted to
hold water.
This helps when it does not rain.

Goldenrod plants
have stiff stems and
leaves. This helps the
plants keep the water
they need to live.

Trees are plants.
Some trees have flowers.
Peach trees grow flowers.
The flowers make peaches.
Peaches are fruits.
Fruits cover peach seeds and keep
them safe.

Plants without Flowers

Some plants do not have flowers.
Some plants have cones.
The seeds grow inside the cones.
The cone opens and seeds fall out.
The seeds grow into new trees.

Pine trees have
cones with seeds.

The stinging nettle has
sharp hairs to help keep
it safe from animals that
want to eat it.

The fanwort is adapted
to live in water.

Plants that Live Near Water

Some plants in a woodland environment
live near water.
These plants are adapted to live where
it is wet.

This red plant is called a cardinal plant.
Its roots are adapted to get nutrients
from wet soil.

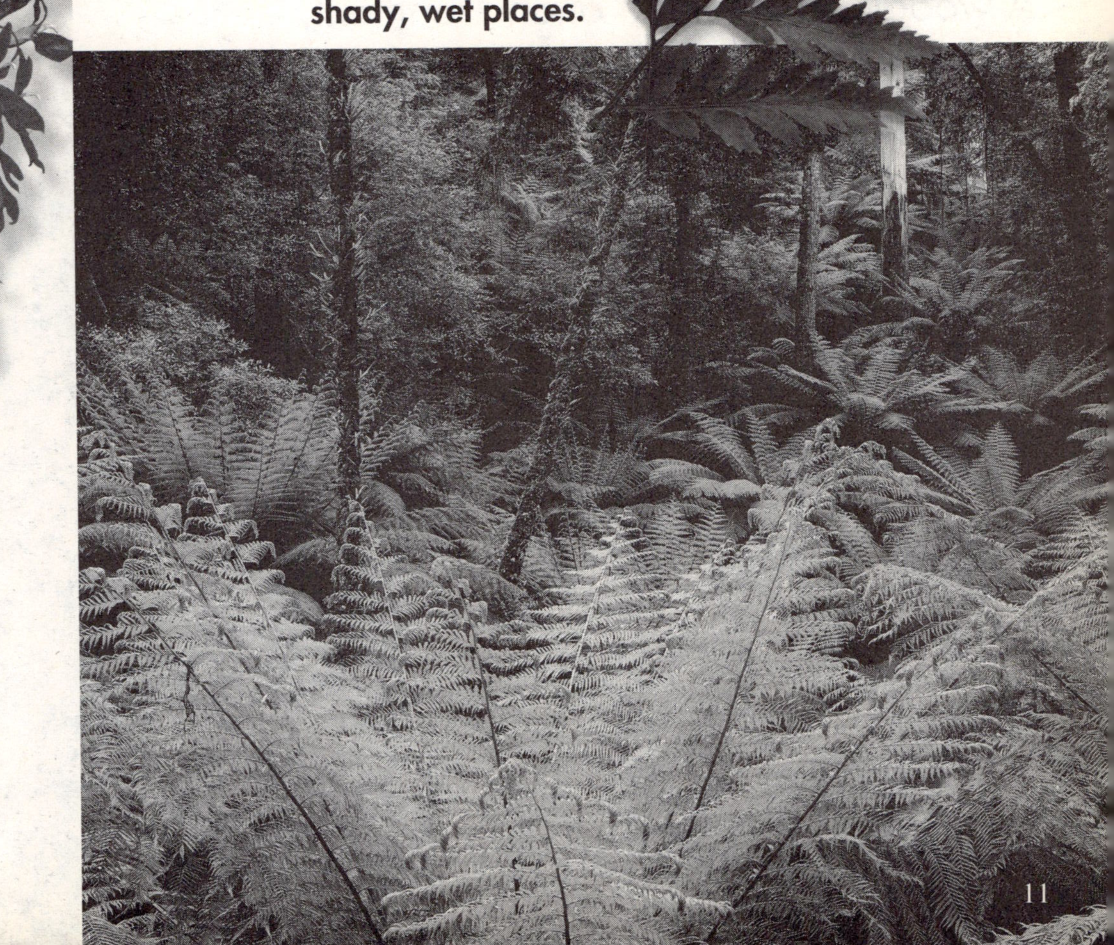

Cardinal plant

Ferns do not have flowers.
Ferns do not make seeds.
Ferns have leaves, roots, and stems.

Ferns live in warm,
shady, wet places.

How are some woodland plants adapted?

Living things have **adapted,** or changed, to live in many places.
An **environment** is a place with living and nonliving things.

A woodland is a kind of environment.
Pine trees are adapted to the cold.

Maple trees are adapted to warm summers and cold winters.
Maple trees have big, flat leaves.
These leaves drop off in the fall.
This helps the tree store water for the winter.

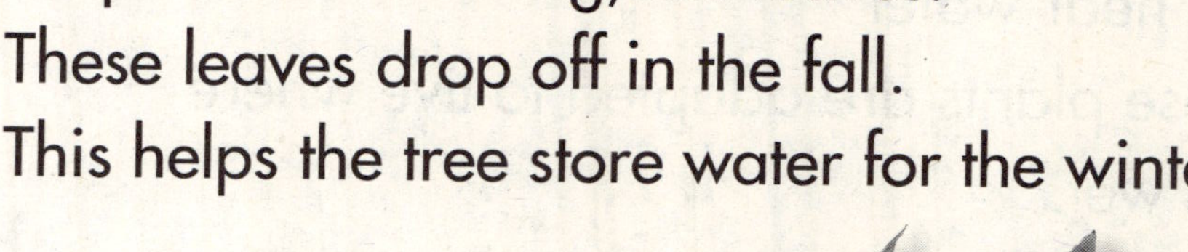

Science Science

All About Animals
by May Evans

Genre	Comprehension Skills	Text Features	Science Content
Nonfiction	Alike and Different	• Glossary	Vertebrates and Invertebrates

Scott Foresman Science 2.2

PEARSON
Scott Foresman

scottforesman.com

ISBN 0-328-13772-3

90000

9 780328 137725

What did you learn?

1. What are the two big groups of animals?

2. How does camouflage help animals stay safe?

3. **Writing** in Science How do penguin body parts help penguins live?

4. **Alike and Different** How are birds like fish? How are they different?

Photographs: Every effort has been made to secure permission and provide appropriate credit for photographic material. The publisher deeply regrets any omission and pledges to correct errors called to its attention in subsequent editions. Unless otherwise acknowledged, all photographs are the property of Scott Foresman, a division of Pearson Education. Photo locators denoted as follows: Top (T), Center (C), Bottom (B), Left (L), Right (R) Background (Bkgd) Opener: (Bkgd) Tom Brakefield/Corbis, (TR) Brand X Pictures 1 DK Images; 2 (TL) Joe McDonald/Corbis, (TC) ©George D.Lepp/Corbis, (TR) Getty Images, (CL) ©Tom Brakefield/Corbis, (CR) Getty Images; 3 ©W. Perry Conway/Corbis; 4 ©Don Enger/Animals Animals/ Earth Scenes; 5 Getty Images; 6 ©Joe McDonald/Animals Animals/Earth Scenes; 7 ©Tom Brakefield/ Corbis; 8 (BL, BR) ©Royalty-Free/Corbis; 9 ©Breck P. Kent/Animals Animals/Earth Scenes; 10 ©Jean-Louis Le Moigne/NHPA Limited; 11–13 DK Images; 14 ©Stephen Dalton/NHPA Limited; 15 ©Daniel Heuclin/ NHPA Limited, (BR) ©Stephen Dalton/NHPA Limited; 16 ©Carmela Leszczynski/Animals Animals/Earth Scenes; 17 ©Kim Taylor/Bruce Coleman Collection; 18 OSF/D. Clyne/Animals Animals/Earth Scenes; 19 DK Images; 20 ©Geoff Moon/Frank Lane Picture Agency/Corbis; 21 DK Images; 22 ©Niall Benvie/ Corbis; 23 ©Tom Brakefield/Corbis

ISBN: 0-328-13772-3

Copyright © Pearson Education, Inc.

All Rights Reserved. Printed in the United States of America. The blackline masters in this publication are designed for use with appropriate equipment to reproduce copies for classroom use only. Scott Foresman grants permission to classroom teachers to reproduce from these masters.

2 3 4 5 6 7 8 9 10 V004 13 12 11 10 09 08 07 06 05

All About Animals

by May Evans

Glossary

amphibian an animal with a backbone and smooth, wet skin that lives on land and in water

bird an animal with a backbone, feathers, and wings that hatches from an egg

camouflage a color or shape that makes an animal hard to see

fish an animal with a backbone, scales, and fins that lives in water

gills body parts that help fish get oxygen from water

insect an animal with three body parts and six legs that does not have a backbone

mammal an animal with a backbone that has hair or fur and gets milk from its mother

reptile an animal with a backbone and scales that hatches from an egg

What are some animals with backbones?

There are many kinds of animals.
Some animal have backbones.
Bones give animals shape.
Bones help animals move.
Bones help animals stay safe.

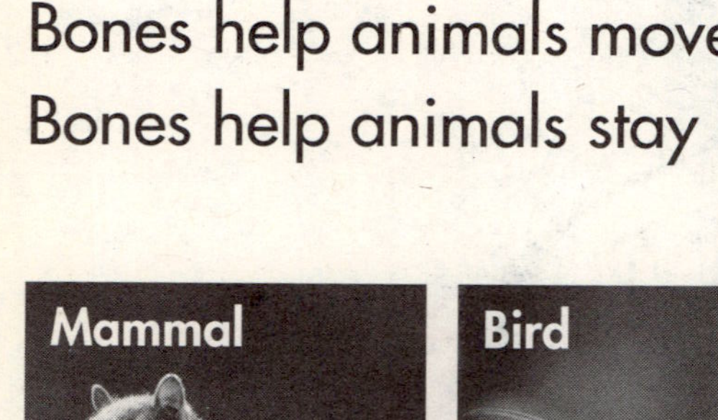

Animals live in many places.
Some animals have backbones.
Some animals do not have backbones.
All animals are adapted to the places
where they live.

Spiders do not have backbones.
Spiders have eight legs.

Spiders make webs.
Insects get into the webs.
Spiders eat the insects.

Animals With Backbones

Mammals have backbones.
Some mammals have fur.
Some mammals have hair.
Young mammals get milk from their mother.

Birds have backbones.
Birds have feathers.
Birds have wings.
Baby birds come from eggs.

Other Animals Without Backbones

This octopus does not have a backbone.

It lives in the ocean.
It can see well in the water.
This helps it find food.

This insect is called a walking stick.
It is hard to see when it is near plants.
Camouflage helps it stay safe.

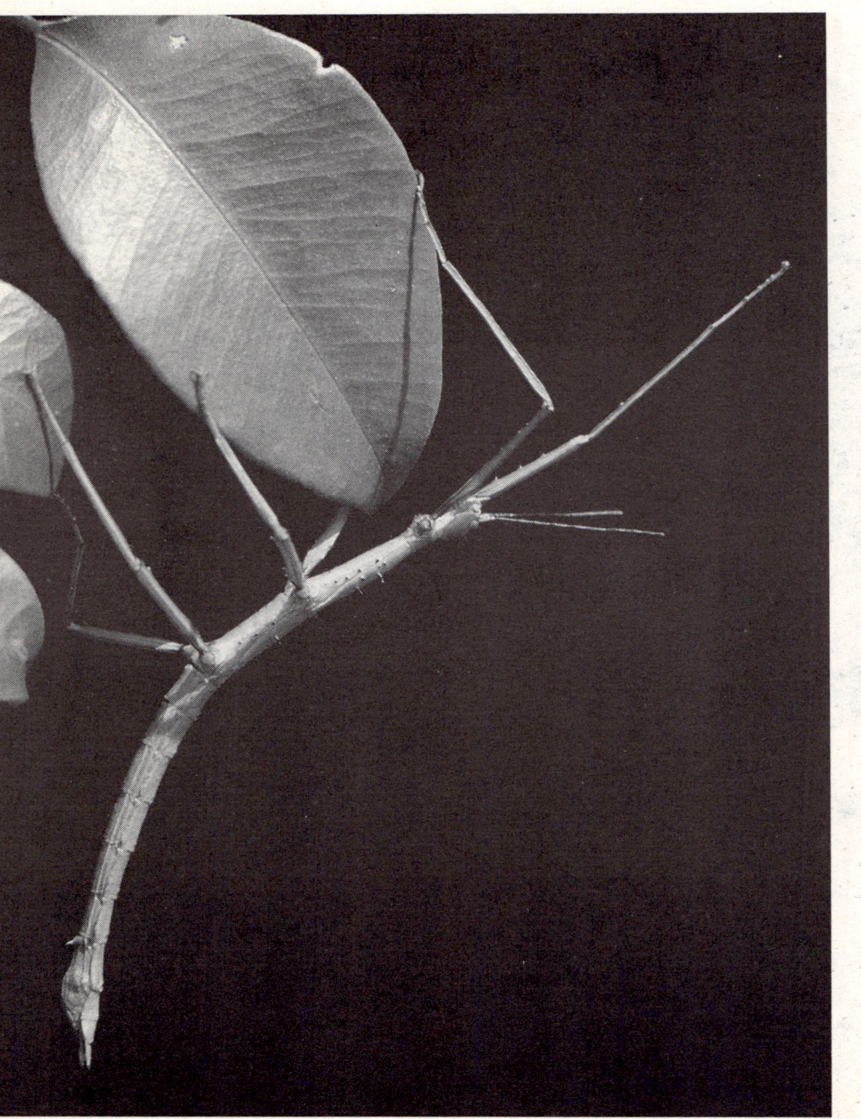

Fish have backbones.
Fish live in water.
Most fish have scales.
Fish have fins.
Fins help fish swim.
Most fish come from eggs.

Reptiles have backbones.
Reptiles also have scales.
Scales help reptiles stay safe.
Some reptiles come from eggs.
Snakes are reptiles.

Insects do not have backbones.
Insects have three body parts and six legs.
Antennae help some insects feel, smell, hear,
and taste.

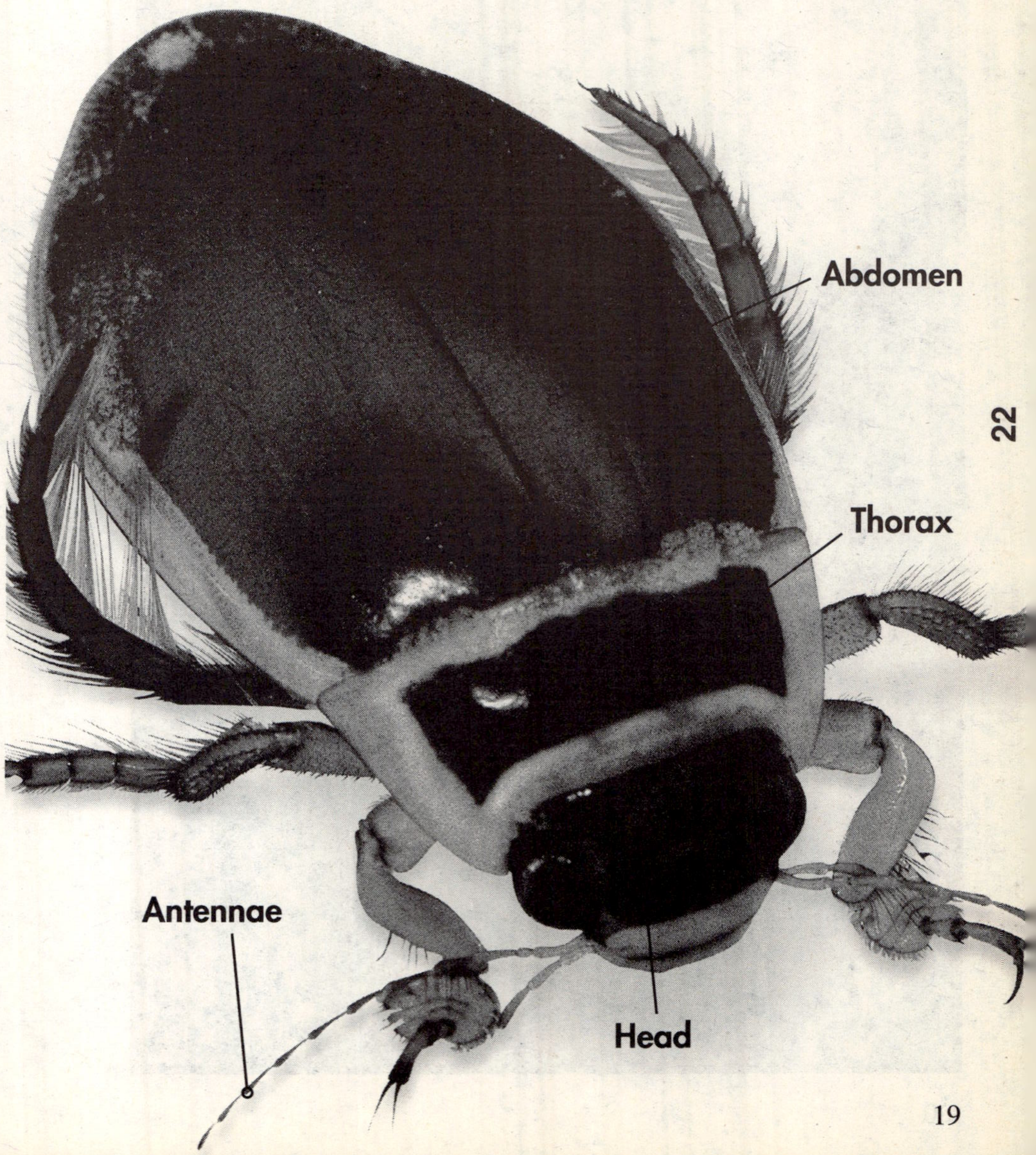

22

What are some animals without backbones?

You now know about animals with backbones.
Another group of animals does not have backbones.
Most animals are in this group.

Honey pot ants

Amphibians have backbones.
Amphibians can live on land.
They can also live in water.

Amphibians have wet skin.
The skin is smooth.
Amphibians come from eggs.

Frogs are amphibians.

What are some ways mammals are adapted?

Mammals live in many different places.
Mammals are adapted to where they live.

This deer's fur changes color in the winter.
Then the deer is hard to see.
This is called camouflage.
Camouflage helps keep this animal safe.

Toads live on land.
They dig into the ground to stay cool.
Toads look for food at night.

What are some ways amphibians are adapted?

Amphibians live in many different places.
First they live in water.
Then they live on land.
Their smooth, wet skin helps them live
in both places.

Animals act in different ways.
Chipmunks store food in the summer.
They sleep in the winter.
When they wake up, they eat the food
they saved.

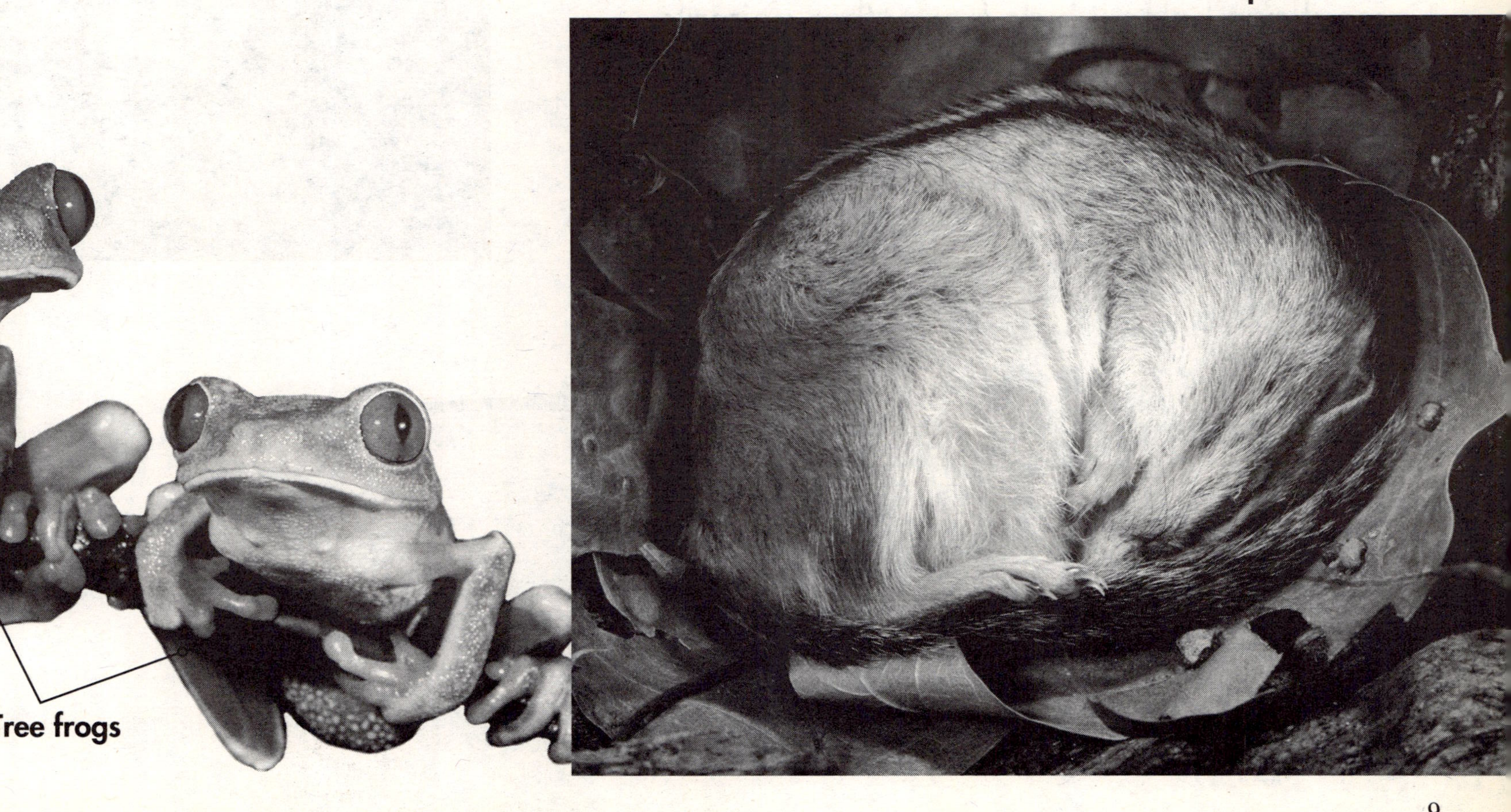

Chipmunk

What are some ways birds are adapted?

Birds live in many different places.
Birds are adapted to where they live.

This bird is hard to see in the forest.
It uses camouflage to stay safe.
Camouflage helps it hide from other animals.

Snakes do not chew their food.
Snakes can open their mouths very wide.
Some snakes swallow their food whole!

Penguins live where it is cold.
They have feathers to keep them warm.

Penguins do not fly.
They use their wings to swim.

What are some ways reptiles are adapted?

Reptiles live in many different places.
Reptiles are cold when it is cold.
Reptiles are warm when it is warm.
Reptiles move fast when they are warm.

This animal lives where it is hot.
It has light skin.
Light skin helps it keep cool.

Chameleon

What are some ways fish are adapted?

Fish live in water.
Fish have gills.
Gills help fish get oxygen from the water.

This catfish swims in deep, dark water.
Long feelers help a catfish find food.

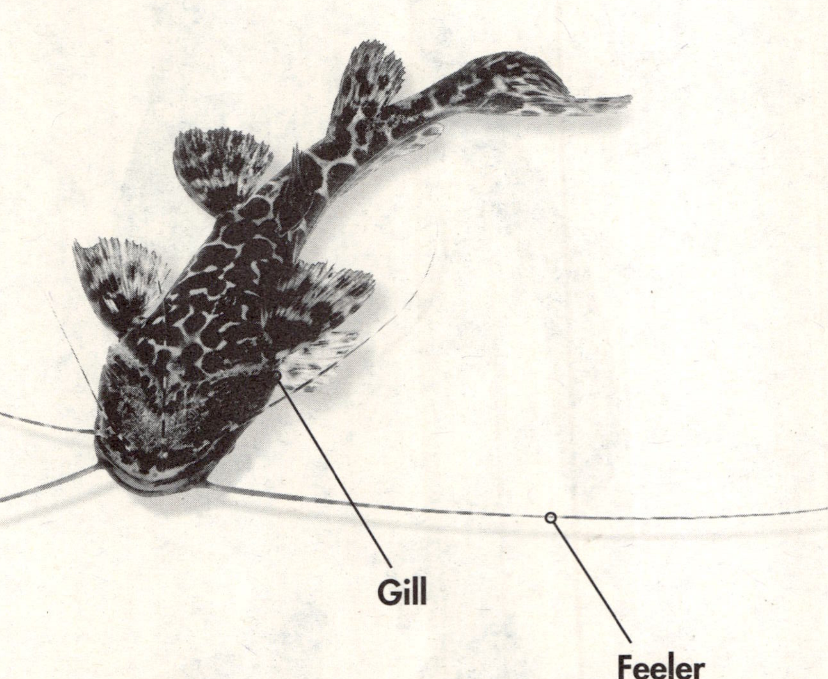

This fish can protect itself.
The fish can make itself big.
This scares away other animals.
The fish changes shape to stay safe.

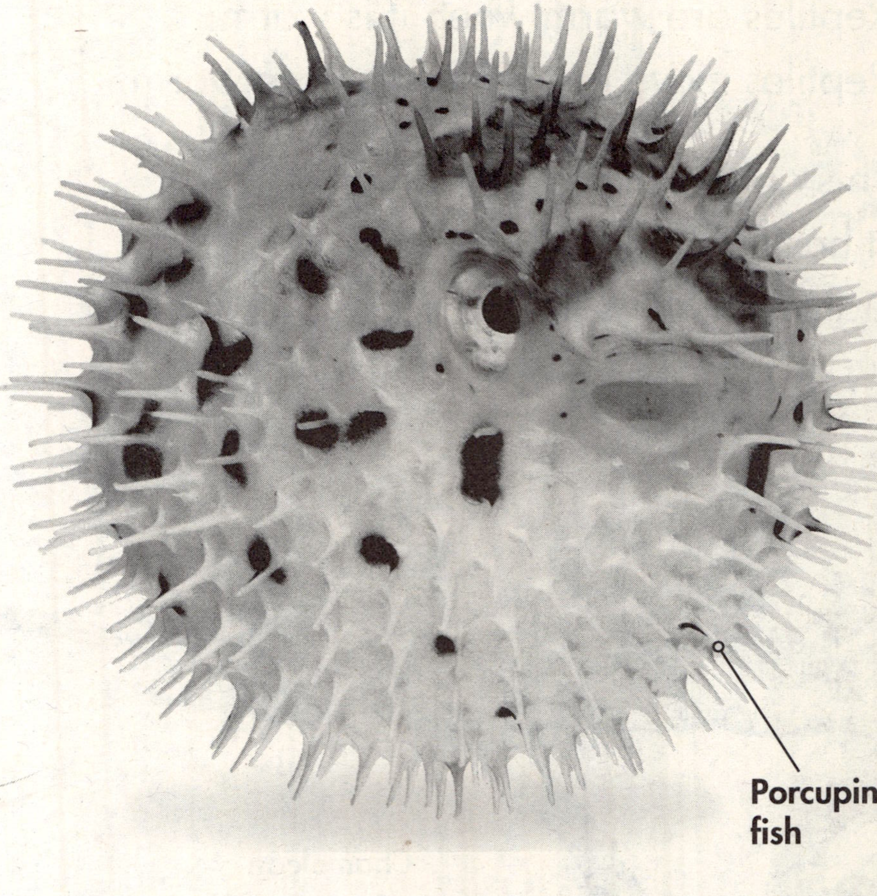

28

How Plants and Animals Live Together

Live Together

by May Evans

29

Genre	Comprehension Skill	Text Features	Science Content
Nonfiction	Cause and Effect	• Diagrams • Glossary	Ecosystems

Scott Foresman Science 2.3

Vocabulary

consumer

food chain

food web

predator

prey

producer

What did you learn?

1. What do plants and animals need?

2. What is a predator?

3. **Writing** in Science Sometimes animals keep each other safe. Write to explain how this happens. Use words from the book as you write.

4. **Cause and Effect** What can cause changes to a food web? What effect did the oil spill have on the sea otters on page 15?

Glossary

consumer — an animal that cannot make its own food but gets it from its habitat

food chain — how energy flows from the Sun to plants to animals in a habitat

food web — many food chains in one place

predator — an animal that hunts and eats other animals

prey — an animal that gets eaten by other animals

producer — a living thing that makes its own food

How Plants and Animals Live Together

by May Evans

What do plants and animals need?

Plants are living things.
Plants need air and water.
Plants need light from the Sun.
Plants need space.

Plants are producers.
A **producer** makes its own food.

Plants and animals live together in
their habitats.
They need each other in many
different ways.

A remora fish swims with a shark.
The shark keeps the remora fish safe.
It scares away predators.

The remora fish needs the shark.
The shark does not hurt the remora fish.

Animals are living things too.
Animals need air and water.
Animals need shelter.
Animals need space.

Animals are consumers.
A **consumer** cannot make its own food.
A consumer gets food from its habitat.

Different Needs

Plants and animals live together.
Plants and animals need each other.

Plants and animals get what they need from
the places they live.

This boxer crab can stay safe near
a sea anemone.
A sea anemone is an animal.
The sea anemone can sting predators that
want to get the boxer crab.

Animals Need Each Other

Sometimes animals help each other get food.
Sometimes animals keep other animals safe.

This bird eats bugs that might hurt the rhino.

Big animals need a lot of food and space.
Small animals need less food and space.

If there is not enough food and space, some animals may die.

How do plants and animals get food in a grassland?

Most plants make food.
Some animals eat plants for food.
Other animals eat these animals.
This is a **food chain.**

All food chains start with the Sun.
Plants get energy from the Sun.
Plants use energy to make food.

This squirrel's nest has twigs and leaves on
the outside.
The twigs and leaves come from plants.
This nest has feathers and wool on
the inside.
The feathers and wool come from animals.

Building Nests

Some animals use plant parts to make nests.
Some animals use animal parts to
make nests.

Animals eat the plants and other animals.
Energy goes from the Sun to the animals.

All food chains have predators.
A **predator** hunts and eats other animals.

All food chains have **prey.**
Predators eat prey.
Prey is the food of predators.

Coyote

Mountain lion

Food Web in a Grassland

Places can have more than one food chain.
A **food web** is many food chains in
one place.

A grassland has many food chains.
They make up a food web.

Cardinal fish live near sea urchins.
The sea urchin's spines stop other animals
from eating the fish.
Cardinal fish do not help or hurt the
sea urchins.

How do plants and animals help each other?

Plants and animals can help each other.
Animals can use plants for shelter.
The animals can help the plants too.

An ant makes its home on an acacia plant.
The ant helps the plant stay safe.
It bites any animal that tries to eat the plant.

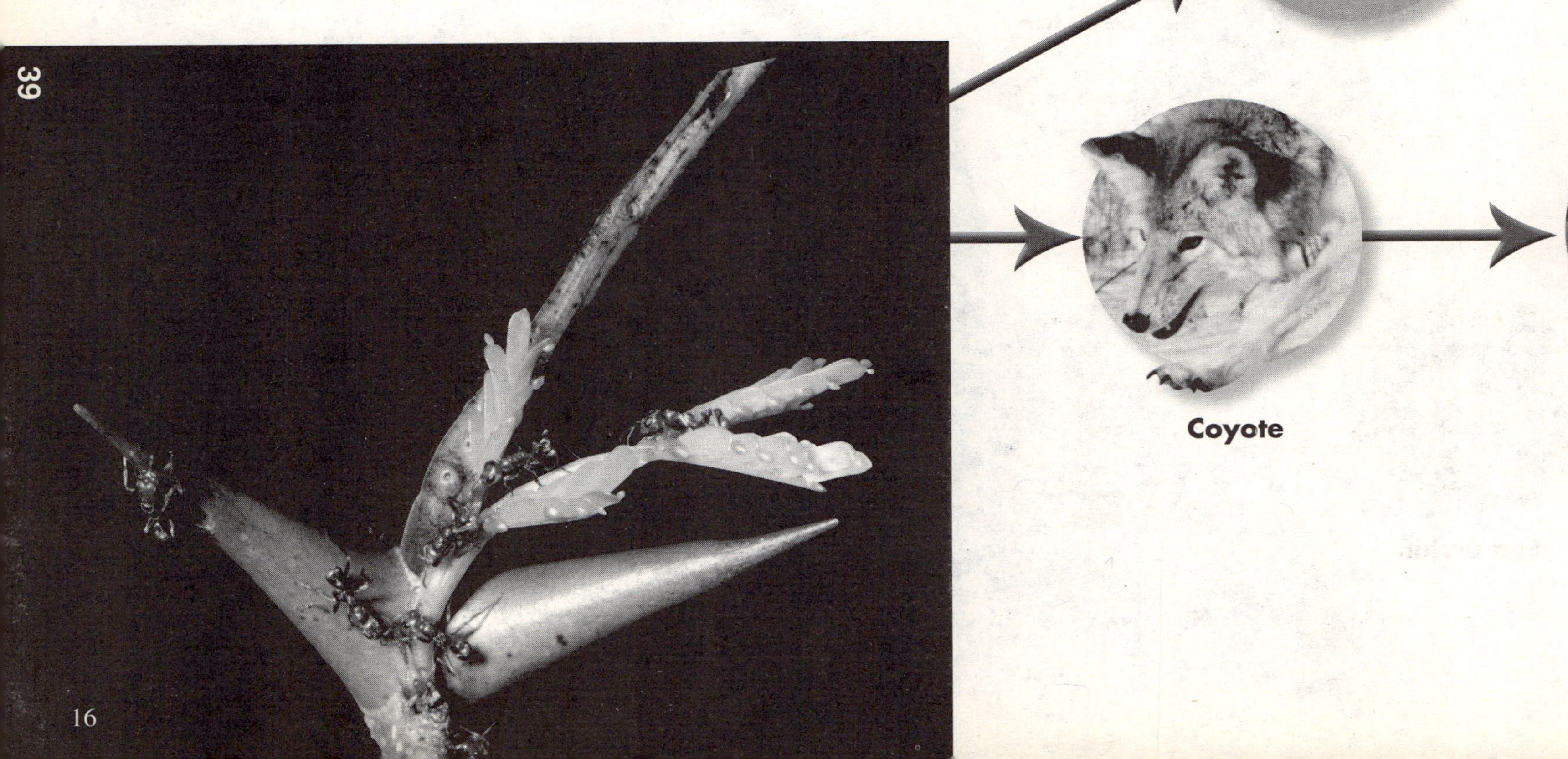

Look at the arrows in this food web.
How many animals eat corn?
How many animals eat voles?

Living things in a food web need each other for energy.

How do plants and animals get food in an ocean?

An ocean has food chains and food webs.

Kelp starts an ocean food chain.
Kelp is an ocean plant.
It uses light from the Sun to make food.

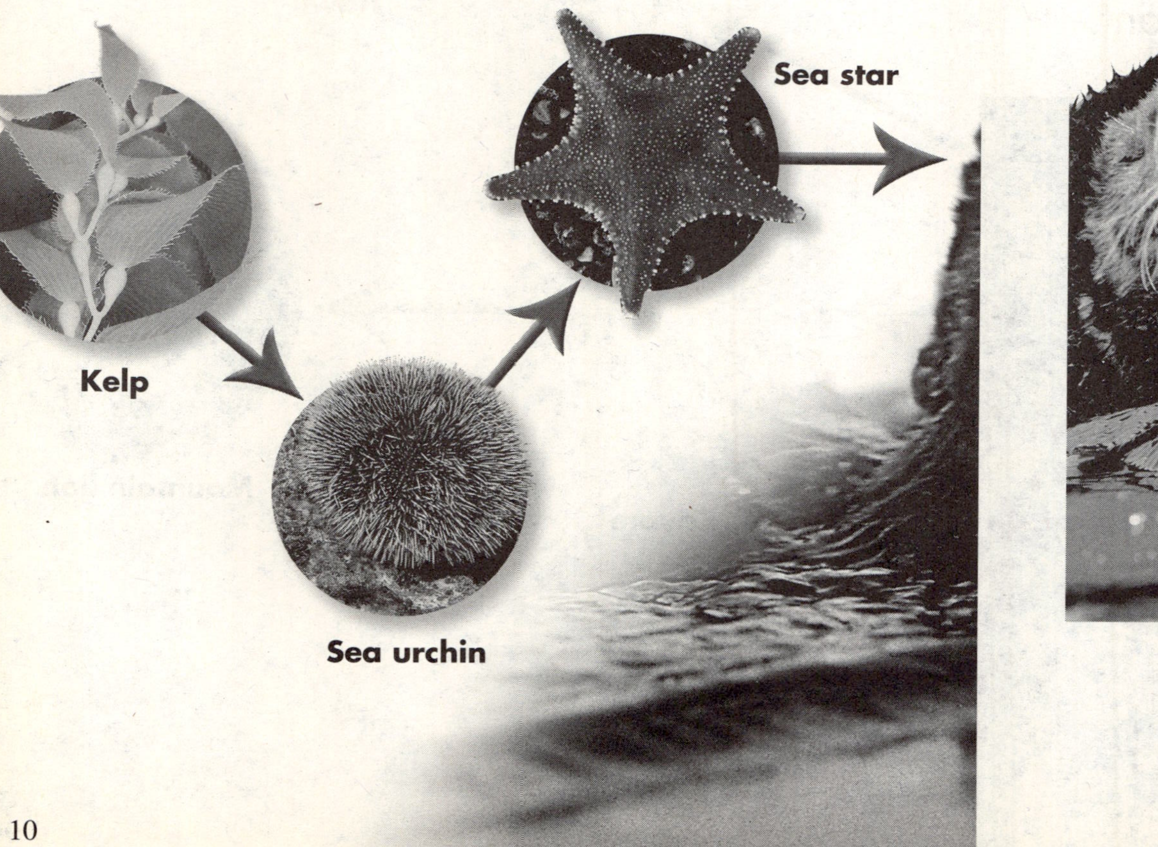

Look at these sea otters.
Sea otters have fur.
The sea otters' fur was hurt by the oil.
People cleaned the sea otters.
They also cleaned the water.
People made the ocean safe again.

What can cause a food web to change?

Many things can change a food web.
Changes can hurt plants and animals.

Some changes are caused by people.
The oil from a ship spilled into the ocean.

The sea urchin gets energy when it eats the kelp.
The sea star gets energy when it eats the sea urchin.
Energy from the Sun goes to all the plants and animals in the ocean.

Sea otter

A Food Web in an Ocean

There are many food chains in an ocean.
They make up ocean food webs.

Look at this picture of an ocean food web.
Which animals eat kelp?
How many animals eat sea urchins?

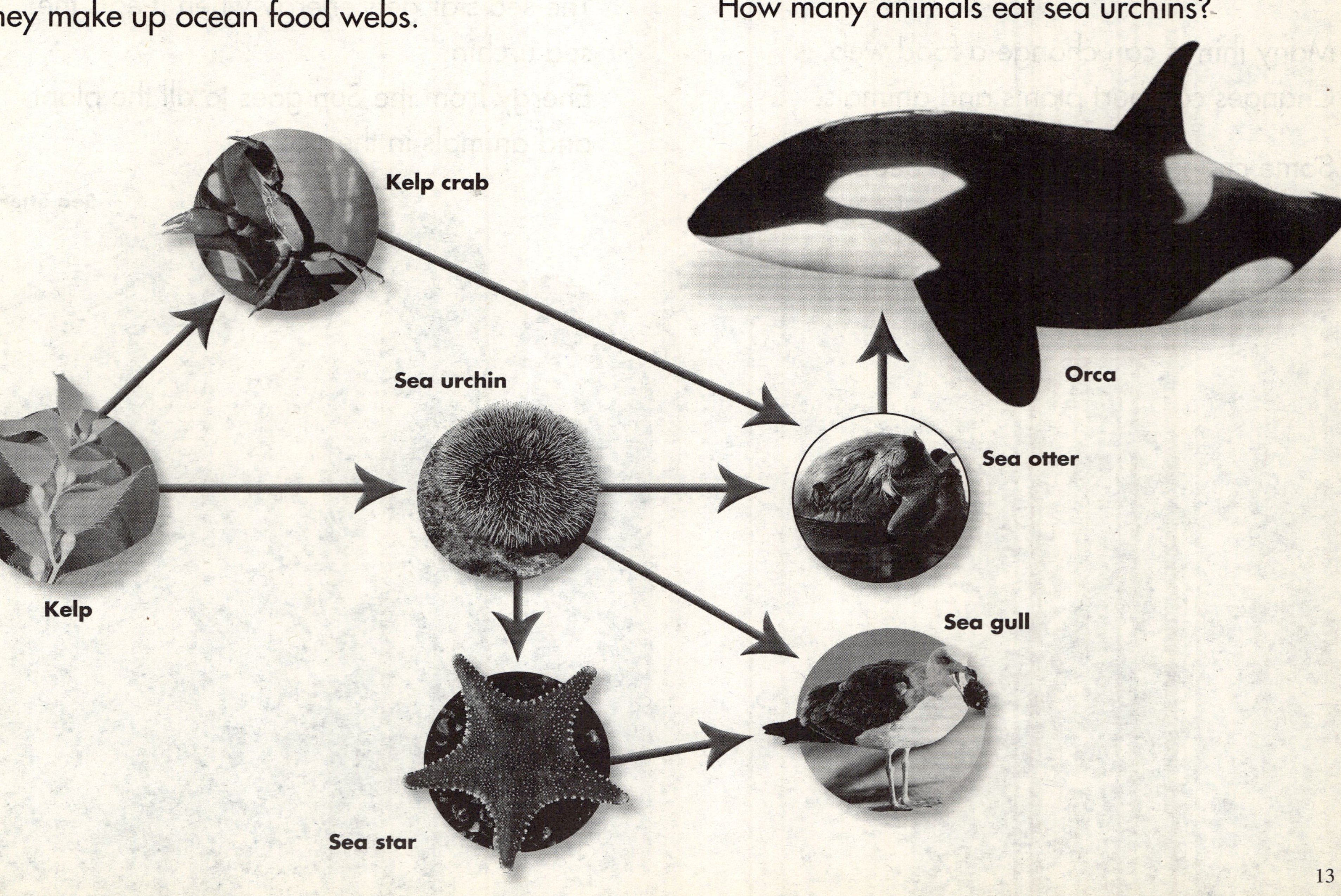

How Living Things Grow and Change

by Rose Murray

Genre	Comprehension Skill	Text Features	Science Content
Nonfiction	Infer	• Captions • Glossary	Living Things

Scott Foresman Science 2.4

43

Science

Science

PEARSON
Scott Foresman

scottforesman.com

DK

ISBN 0-328-13778-2

9 780328 137787

90000

What did you learn?

1. What is a life cycle?

2. Which animals in this book start as eggs?

3. **Writing** in Science Young giraffes look different from adult giraffes. Write to explain how they are different. Use words from the book as you write.

4. **Infer** One seed gets water and air. One seed does not. What will happen to the seeds? Why?

Photographs: Every effort has been made to secure permission and provide appropriate credit for photographic material. The publisher deeply regrets any omission and pledges to correct errors called to its attention in subsequent editions. Unless otherwise acknowledged, all photographs are the property of Scott Foresman, a division of Pearson Education. Photo locators denoted as follows: Top (T), Center (C), Bottom (B), Left (L), Right (R) Background (Bkgd)

Opener: (Bkgd) ©Andy Rouse/NHPA Limited, (TR) ©Paul A. Sounders/Corbis; Title Page: ©Gary W. Carter/Corbis; 2 (Bkgd) ©Tom Brakefield/Corbis; 4 (Bkgd) ©Peter Johnson/Corbis; 5 (CR) ©Jonathan Blair/Corbis, (BR) ©C. Allan Morgan/Peter Arnold, Inc.; 6 (CC) ©Jonathan Blair/Corbis, (BL) ©Soames Summerhays/Photo Researchers, Inc.; 7 ©DK Images; 8 (CC) ©DK Images, (BL) Robert Thompson/NHPA Limited; 9 ©DK Images; 10 Bob Langrish/©DK Images; 11(BL, BR) ©DK Images; 12 (CC) ©Tim Davis/ Corbis; 13 (B) ©Kevin Schafer/NHPA Limited; 14 (BL, BR) ©DK Images; 15 ©DK Images; 16 (BC) ©Taxi/ Getty Images, (R) ©Robert Landau/Corbis; 17 ©DK Images; 18 ©DK Images; 19 (BL, BC, CR) ©DK Images; 20 (CL, BR) ©DK Images; 21 ©DK Images; 22 (B) ©Andy Rouse/NHPA Limited.

ISBN: 0-328-13778-2

How Living Things Grow and Change

by Rose Murray

Glossary

germinate to start growing

life cycle how a living thing grows and changes

nymph a young insect

seed coat a hard cover on a seed

seedling a young plant

How do sea turtles grow and change?

Living things need food and water.
Some living things can move.
Living things grow and change.

Living things can be like their parents.
They can be different.
All living things have life cycles.
All living things grow and change.

Animals are living things.
Plants are living things.
Some living things can be parents.

Animals and plants are living things.
At first they are small.
Then they grow bigger.
Animals and plants need food to grow
and change.

Sea Turtle Eggs

A sea turtle is an ocean animal.
It digs a hole in the sand.
It lays eggs in the hole.

People in families can look like each other.
People in families can look different from each other too.

How People Are Different

People can be short or tall.
People can have brown eyes.
People can have blue eyes.
Their hair can be different.
Their skin color can be different.

The eggs lie in the sand for two months.
Then they hatch.

Baby turtles have an egg tooth.
They use the egg tooth to get out of the egg.
Later, the tooth falls out.

The Life Cycle of a Sea Turtle

A **life cycle** is the way a living thing
grows and changes.
Look at the life cycle of this sea turtle.

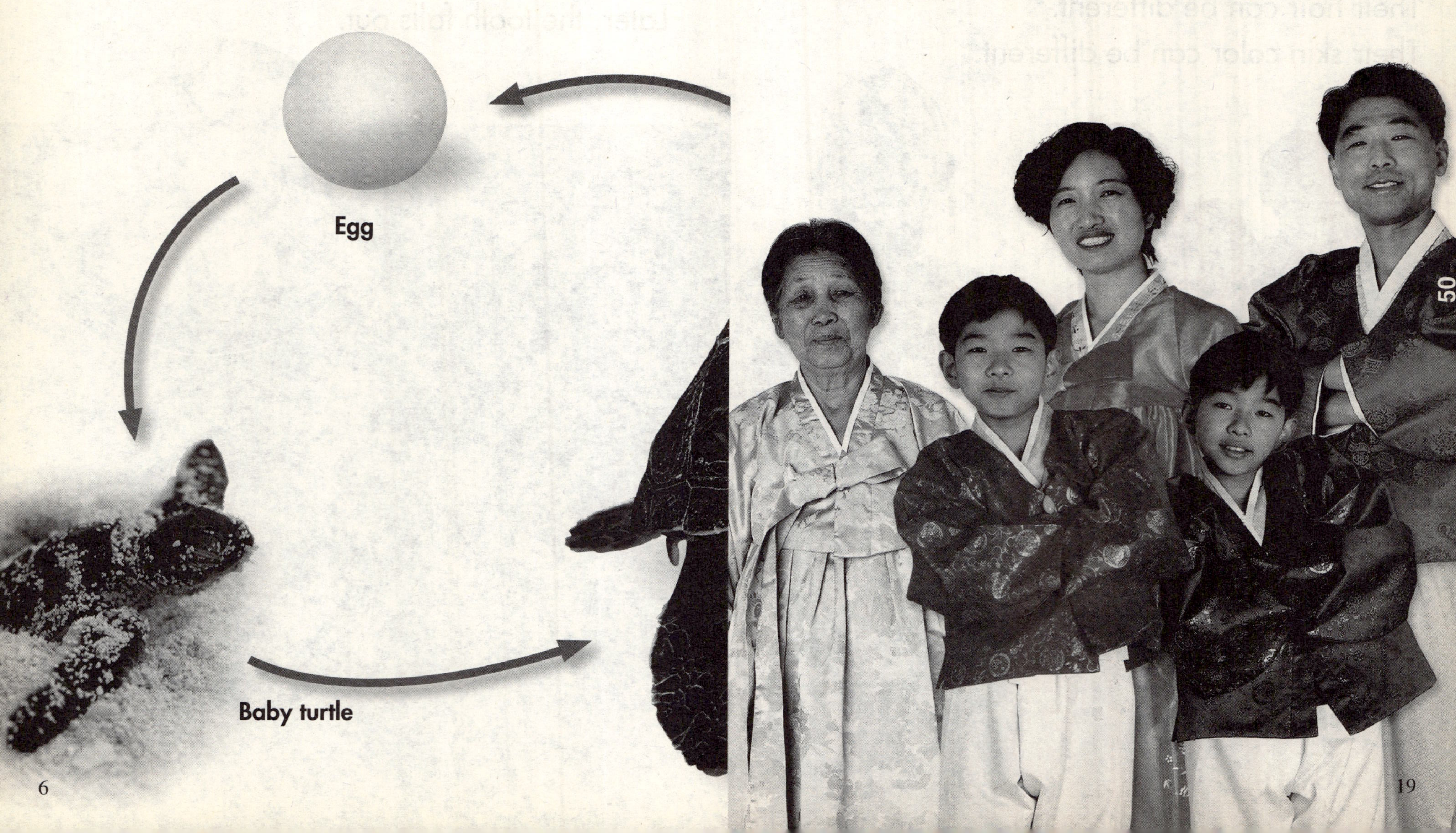

One day you will be a teenager.
Then you will be a grown-up.

Grown-ups change too.
The color of their hair may change.

The grown-up turtle can lay eggs.
It can start a new life cycle.

Grown-up turtle

How do people grow and change?

People change as they grow.
You used to be a baby.
Now you are a child.
You grew tall.
You learned how to talk.
You learned how to read.

What is the life cycle of a dragonfly?

Insects have life cycles.
Insects start as eggs.
Many baby insects are called **nymphs.**
Nymphs look like their parents
without wings.
Nymphs shed their hard skin as they grow.

Small foxgloves do not have flowers.
They grow for two years.
Then they grow flowers.

How are young plants like their parents?

Small plants can look like their parents.
They can be the same color.
They can be the same shape.
They can look different in some ways too.

A young saguaro cactus does not have arms. The cactus starts to grow arms when it is very old.

Dragonflies lay eggs in water.
Nymphs come out of the eggs.
Nymphs grow up.
Then they can lay eggs.
Now the life cycle starts again.

Grown-up dragonfly

What is the life cycle of a horse?

A horse is a mammal.
Mammals have a life cycle.
Baby mammals grow in their mothers.
They get milk from their mothers.

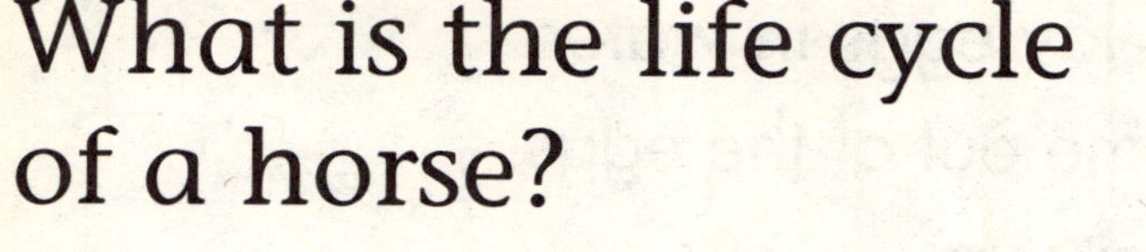

Roots will grow down.
A stem will grow up.
This is called a **seedling.**
A seedling is a small plant.

One day a seedling will be a big plant.
It will grow flowers and seeds.
Then the life cycle will start again.

What is the life cycle of a bean plant?

Plants grow from seeds.
A seed is the start of a plant life cycle.
A seed has a cover called a **seed coat.**
The seed coat keeps the seed safe.

A seed has a tiny plant in it.
A seed holds food inside.
The tiny plant needs water and air too.
Then it will **germinate,** or grow.

A baby horse is called a foal.
It looks like its parents.
When a foal grows up it can have new foals.
Then the life cycle starts again.

How are young animals like their parents?

Baby animals can look like their parents.
They can be the same shape.
They can be the same color.
Baby animals can be different in some
ways too.

All giraffes have spots.
The spots on a grown-up giraffe are dark.
The spots on a baby giraffe are not as dark.

Earth's Land, Air, and Water

by Emily McKenzie

Genre	Comprehension Skill	Text Features	Science Content
Nonfiction	Picture Clues	• Labels • Glossary	Natural Resources

Scott Foresman Science 2.5

ISBN 0-328-13781-2

90000

9 780328 137817

Vocabulary

boulder

erosion

minerals

natural resource

pollution

recycle

sand

weathering

What did you learn?

1. What is soil made of?

2. Name three natural resources.

3. **Writing** in Science People need to be careful with campfires. In your own words, write to explain why.

4. **Picture Clues** Look at the picture on page 6. Can you point to the boulder?

Photographs: Every effort has been made to secure permission and provide appropriate credit for photographic material. The publisher deeply regrets any omission and pledges to correct errors called to its attention in subsequent editions. Unless otherwise acknowledged, all photographs are the property of Scott Foresman, a division of Pearson Education. Photo locators denoted as follows: Top (T), Center (C), Bottom (B), Left (L), Right (R) Background (Bkgd)
Opener: (TR) ©Stone/Getty Images, (Bkgd) ©Steve Terrill/Corbis, (Bkgd) ©M. Colbeck/OSF/Animals Animals/Earth Scenes; Title Page: (Bkgd) ©Steve Terrill/Corbis 3 (T) ©Steve Terrill/Corbis, (B) ©Donna Disario/Corbis; 4 (TR) ©Roy Morsch/Corbis, (BL) ©DK Images; 5 ©Craig Tuttle/Corbis; 6 (BR) ©DK Images, ©Royalty-Free/Corbis; 8 ©David M. Dennis/Animals Animals/Earth Scenes; 10 (BR) ©Royalty-Free/Corbis; 11 ©Royalty-Free/Corbis; 12 ©Grant Heilman/Grant Heilman Photography; 13 ©Lester Lefkowitz/Corbis; 14 (B) ©Charles E. Rotker/Corbis, ©Gary Meszaros/Visuals Unlimited; 16 ©Eric Fowke/PhotoEdit; 17 ©Pete Soloutos/Corbis; 18 (TR) ©Ryan McVay/PhotoDisc, (CC) ©Pete Soloutos/Corbis, (BR) ©ThinkStock/SuperStock; 19 ©Steve Terrill/Corbis; 21 Digital Vision; 22 (BL) ©Phil Schermeister/Corbis, (CR) ©Photodisc Red/Getty Images; 23 ©Momatiuk Eastcott/Animals Animals/Earth Scenes.

ISBN: 0-328-13781-2

Copyright © Pearson Education, Inc.

2 3 4 5 6 7 8 9 10 V004 13 12 11 10 09 08 07 06 05

Glossary

boulder	a large rock
erosion	when wind and rain move soil
minerals	natural resources that make up rocks
natural resource	a material people use that comes from Earth
pollution	putting harmful things into the water, air, or land
recycle	to change something so it can be used again
sand	small pieces of rock
weathering	when water or temperature change the land

Earth's Land, Air, and Water

by Emily McKenzie

What are natural resources?

Natural resources come from Earth.
A **natural resource** is something that
people can use.
Sun, water, and air are natural resources.

A refuge is a safe place for plants
and animals.
People can visit a refuge and enjoy all the
plants and animals living in it.

Earth gives us many natural resources.
Let's enjoy them and help keep them safe!

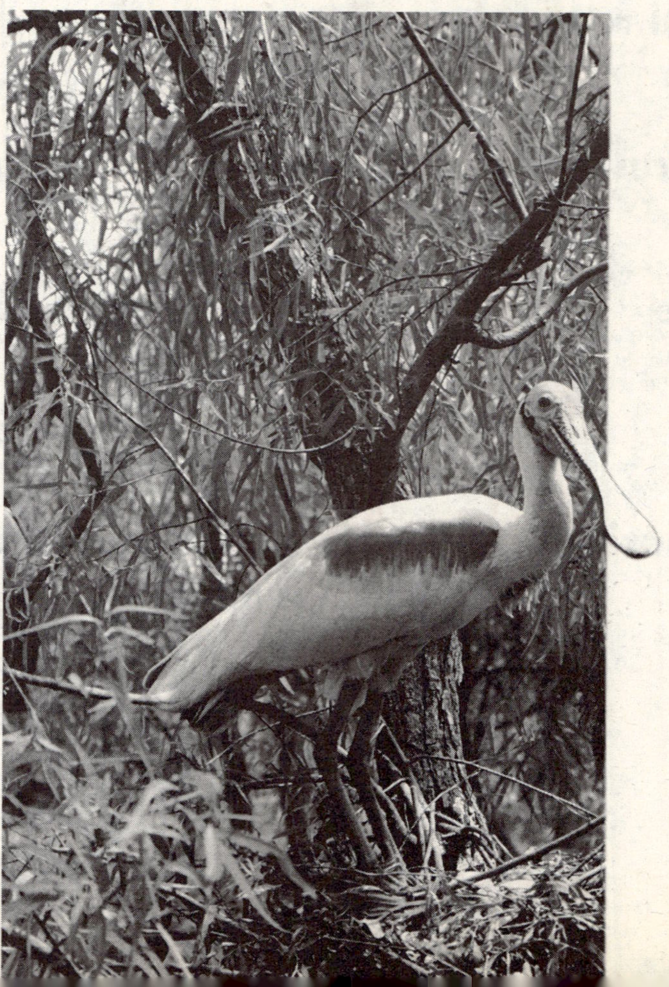

People must be careful with campfires.
Campfires can start a forest fire.
Forest fires can kill many trees and animals.

Plants and animals can also lose their homes
when people build where they live.

Some natural resources can get used up.
Oil and coal are resources that get used up.

Some natural resources can be replaced.
We can plant new trees.

Some natural resources cannot be used up.
Sun, water, and air cannot be used up.

Water and Air

Water is a natural resource.
Plants and animals need water to live.

People need water too.
People use water to drink, cook, and clean.

Forests change all the time.
Trees can burn in forest fires.
The wind can blow down trees.
New trees take a long time to grow back.

Protecting Plants and Animals

People cut down trees.
Animals live in the trees.
The animals lose their homes.
People can plant new trees for the animals.

Ponds and rivers have fresh water.
Oceans have salt water.

Air is a natural resource too.
Plants, animals, and people need air.
Wind is air that moves.

What are rocks and soil like?

Rocks are natural resources.
Rocks can be big or small.
A **boulder** is a very big rock.

Wind, rain, and ice can break up rocks.
Sand is made of small pieces of rock.

People use sand to make roads.
People use rocks to make houses.

People can reduce the natural resources they use.
To reduce means to use less.

People can reuse things to stop pollution.
To reuse means to use over and over again.

Rocks are made up of **minerals.**
Minerals are a natural resource.

Gold and silver are minerals.
Quartz is a mineral.
People make glass from quartz.

Quartz

Soil

Soil covers most of the land.
Soil is a natural resource.
Soil is made of clay, sand, and humus.
It also has air and water in it.

Some animals live in soil.
Different plants grow in different kinds
of soil.

Did you know milk cartons can be recycled?
The milk cartons in this picture were used to
make a playground!

Reduce, Reuse, Recycle

Trash is a kind of pollution.
When we pick up trash, we help stop pollution.

People can recycle trash.
To **recycle** means to change something so that it can be used again.

Sandy soil is found in deserts.
Clay soil is soft and smooth.
Humus is a part of soil that comes from living things.

Clay

Humus

How do people use plants?

Plants are natural resources.
People use plants for many things.
People use wood to build homes and to
make paper.

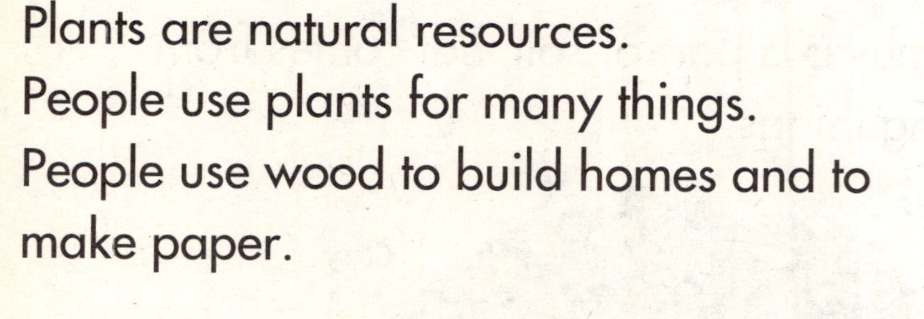

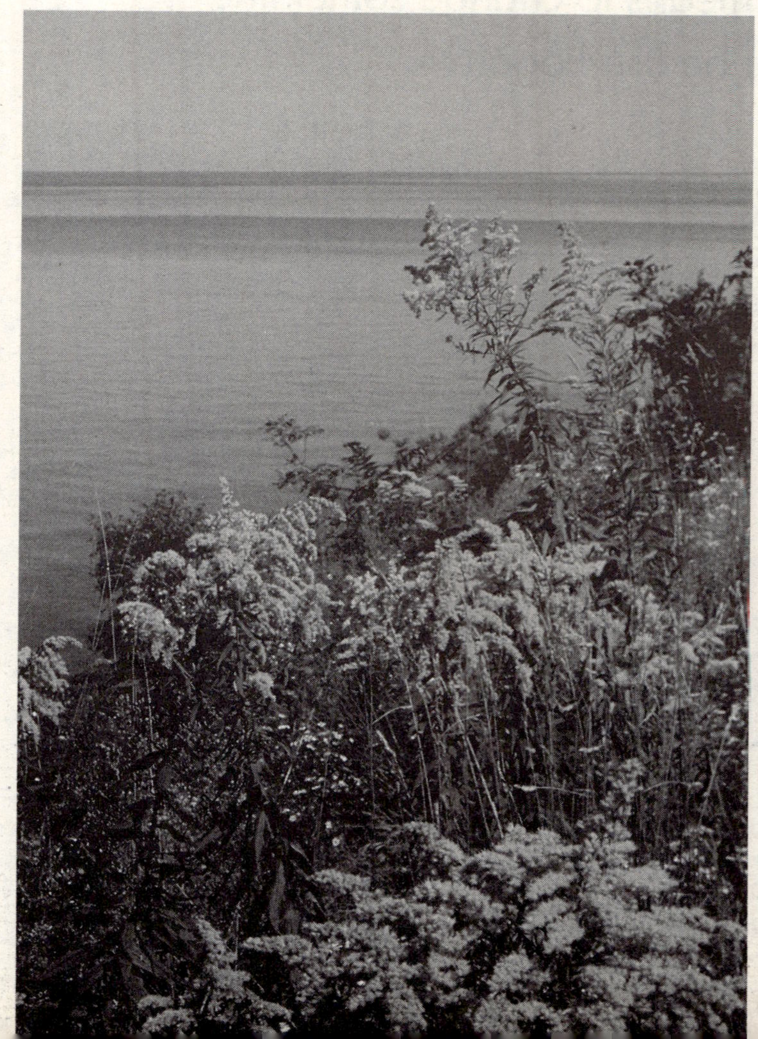

Pollution hurts plants and animals.
People try to stop pollution.
People want to keep Earth clean.
They want to keep plants and animals safe.

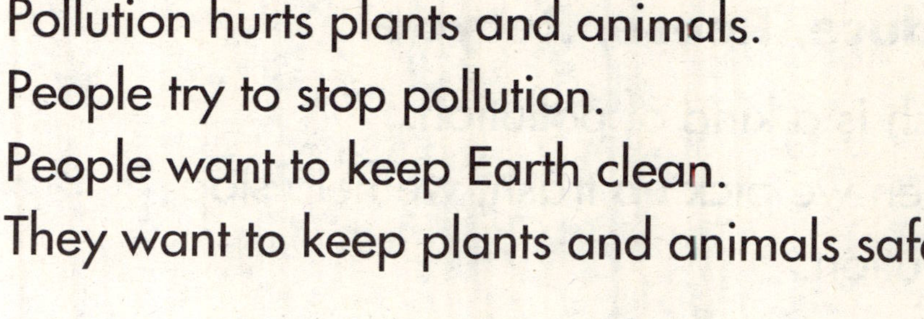

How can people help protect Earth?

People can change Earth.
People can harm the land, air, and water.
This is called **pollution.**

This T-shirt is made from a cotton plant.
People use wheat to make bread.

How does Earth change?

Earth changes all the time.
Water and wind move rocks and soil.
This is called **erosion.**

Plants can stop erosion.
Their roots keep soil in place.

Weather can change Earth.
Water can break up rocks.
This is called **weathering.**

Animals can change Earth.
They dig homes and break up the soil.

Earth's Weather and Seasons

by Ann J. Jacobs

71

Genre	Comprehension Skill	Text Features	Science Content
Nonfiction	Draw Conclusions	• Captions • Diagram • Glossary	Weather

Scott Foresman Science 2.6

What did you learn?

1. What happens to plants in the fall?

2. What do animals do when they *migrate*?

3. **Writing** in Science Water moves in a cycle. Write to explain what this means. Use words from the book as you write.

4. **Draw Conclusions** Which do you think is more dangerous, a thunderstorm or a tornado? Why?

Photographs: Every effort has been made to secure permission and provide appropriate credit for photographic material. The publisher deeply regrets any omission and pledges to correct errors called to its attention in subsequent editions. Unless otherwise acknowledged, all photographs are the property of Scott Foresman, a division of Pearson Education. Photo locators denoted as follows: Top (T), Center (C), Bottom (B), Left (L), Right (R) Background (Bkgd)
Opener: (Bkgd) ©Jim Zuckerman/Corbis; (TC) ©Taxi/Getty Images; ©Macduff Everton/Corbis, (TR) Getty Images; (Bkgd) ©Bill Ross/Corbis; Title Page: ©The Image Bank/Getty Images; 2 (Bkgd) ©Otto Rogge/Corbis, ©Bill Ross/Corbis; 3 © DK Images; 4 (CL) ©Richard Hamilton Smith/Corbis, (CR) ©Phil Schermeister/NGS Image Collection; 5 ©Stone/Getty Images; 6 ©Sam Abell/NGS Image Collection; 8 (B) ©Photographer's Choice/Getty Images, ©Tom Brakefield /Corbis; 9 (BL) ©The Image Bank/Getty Images, (T) ©Dennis MacDonald/PhotoEdit, (BR) ©Taxi/Getty Images; 10 ©John Conrad/Corbis; 11 (TL) ©James Schwabel/Panoramic Images, Chicago, (TR) ©Michael Boys/Corbis, (CC) ©D. Robert and Lorri Franz/Corbis; 12 ©Gary W. Carter/Corbis; 13 (TL) ©Stone/Getty Images, ©Lowell Georgia/Corbis; 14 ©Marty Stoufer/Animals Animals/Earth Scenes; 15 (TL) ©Photographer's Choice/Getty Images, (CL) ©Photodisc Green/Getty Images, (CL) ©Comstock Images/Getty Images; 17 ©A & J Verkaik/Corbis; 19 ©Alan. R. Moller/Getty Images; 21 ©The Image Bank/Getty Images; 22 (BR) ©James Schwabel/ Panoramic Images, Chicago, (T) ©The Image Bank/Getty Images; 23 ©Photodisc Green/Getty Images.

ISBN: 0-328-13784-7

Copyright © Pearson Education, Inc.

All Rights Reserved. Printed in the United States of America. The blackline masters in this publication are designed for use with appropriate equipment to reproduce copies for classroom use only. Scott Foresman grants permission to classroom teachers to reproduce from these masters.

2 3 4 5 6 7 8 9 10 V004 13 12 11 10 09 08 07 06 05

Glossary

condense   to change into small drops of water

evaporate   to change into water vapor

hibernate   to have a long, deep sleep during winter

hurricane   a strong windstorm that starts over warm ocean water

lightning   a flash of light in the sky

migrate   to move to a warmer place

tornado   a strong wind that comes down from the clouds

water cycle   the way water moves from the clouds to Earth and back to the clouds

Earth's Weather and Seasons

by Ann J. Jacobs

What are some kinds of weather?

You wake up.
How do you know what to put on?
Check the weather!

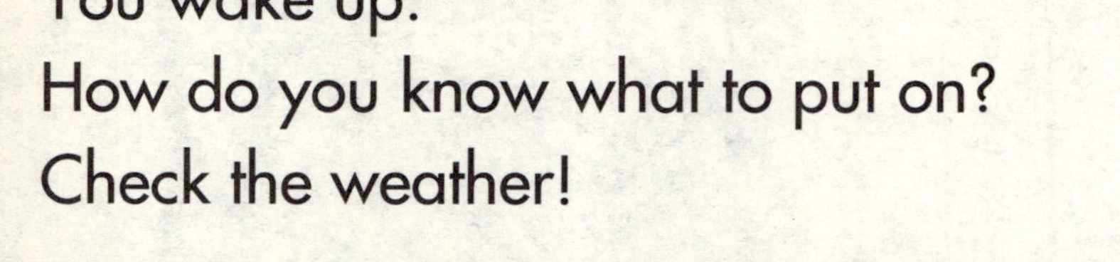

Some weather is not safe.
Some weather is fun.

What is the weather like today?

Weather changes from season to season.
Some weather is wet.
Some weather is dry.
Some weather is hot.
Some weather is cold.

Weather is what it is like outside.
Is it hot, or is it cold?
Look up at the sky.
Look at the tree branches.
Are they moving?
Is there wind?

Flying a kite on a
windy day is fun!

Wet and Dry Weather

Rain, sleet, and snow are all wet weather.
Clouds help tell what kind of weather is
coming.
Clouds are made of many drops of water.
When the clouds get full, the drops fall.

Heavy rains can fall in spring and summer.

Hurricane Safety!

- Move to a place away from the ocean.

- Cover up windows.

- Bring things inside.

- Keep drinking water with you.

- Make sure your flashlight and radio work.

- Stay inside.

- Stay away from windows.

Hurricanes

A **hurricane** is a big storm.
A hurricane starts over warm ocean water.
The rain from a hurricane can make a flood.

A hurricane has strong winds.
The winds can blow down trees and buildings.

Water from clouds can fall as rain, snow, or sleet.
Snow and sleet fall when the air is cold.
Rain falls when the air is warm.

Sometimes rain does not fall for a long time.
This is called a drought.
There is no water for plants and animals when this happens.

Some plants cannot live in a drought.

Some places get snow in winter.

What is the water cycle?

Water moves in a circle.
This is called the **water cycle.**
Water falls from clouds to Earth.
Then it moves back up to the clouds.
Look at the four steps of the water cycle.

 **Tornado Safety!**

- Get inside a closet or a bathroom.

- Sit under the stairs.

- Keep away from windows.

- Keep away from water.

- Keep away from things made of metal and things that are electric.

- Cover your head.

- If you are outside, lie flat on the ground.

Tornadoes

A **tornado** is a very strong wind.
A tornado comes down from the clouds.
It looks like a funnel.

A tornado breaks everything in its path.

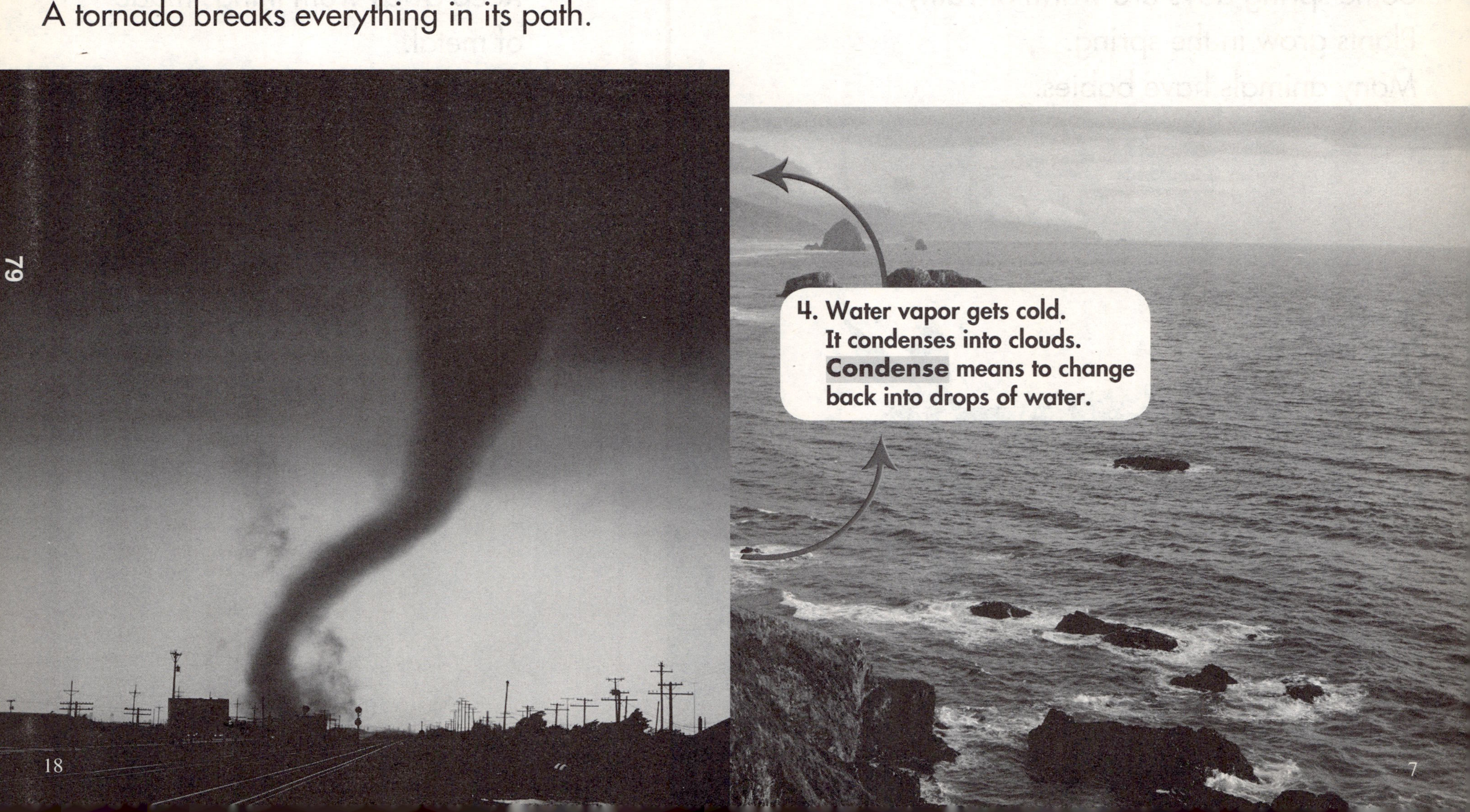

What is spring?

Weather can change with the seasons.

Some spring days are cool.
Some spring days are warm or rainy.
Plants grow in the spring.
Many animals have babies.

**A deer and her
baby in the spring.**

 **Thunderstorm Safety!**

• Go inside.

• Keep away from water.

• Keep away from things made
of metal.

• Do not stand under a tree.

• Do not use a phone.

• Keep away from electrical things.

What are some kinds of bad weather?

A thunderstorm is one kind of bad weather.
A thunderstorm has lots of wind and rain.
A thunderstorm has thunder.
It has lightning.
Lightning is a flash of light in the sky.

What is summer?

Summer comes after spring.
Summer can have hot days and
warm nights.
Green leaves grow on many trees
and plants.
Flowers, fruits, and vegetables grow.

You can see animal
families in the summer.

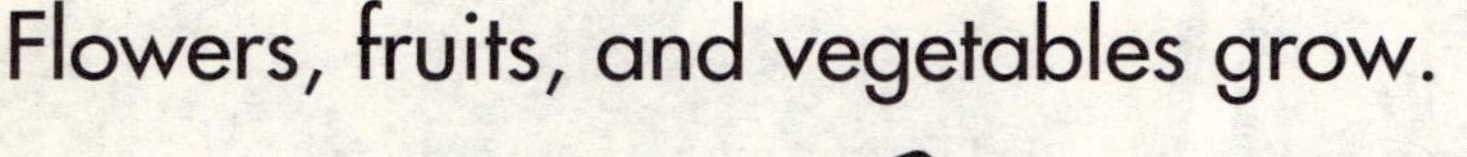

What is winter?

Winter comes after fall.
Winter can be very cold.
It may snow.
Ponds and streams may turn to ice.

Some animals **hibernate.**
They sleep all winter and wake up in
the spring.

Bears hibernate
in the winter.

14

11

What is fall?

Fall comes after summer.
In fall the air gets cooler.
Some leaves change colors.

Some animals look for food for the winter.
Other animals **migrate,** or go to a
warmer place.

In fall, some
animals find food
for the winter.

Fossils and Dinosaurs

by Jennifer Reynolds

Genre	Comprehension Skill	Text Features	Science Content
Nonfiction	Retell	• captions • Labels • Glossary	Fossils and Dinosaurs

Scott Foresman Science 2.7

PEARSON
Scott Foresman

DK

ISBN 0-328-13787-1

90000

9 780328 137879

scottforesman.com

What did you learn?

1. What can paleontologists learn from fossils?

2. What does *extinct* mean?

3. **Writing** in Science Paleontologists changed their minds about Oviraptors when they found new fossils. Write to explain what they thought at different times. Use words from the book as you write.

4. **Retell** In your own words tell about how the lizard fossil on page 4 was formed.

Illustrations: 4, 5, 14 Big Sesh Studios
Photographs: Every effort has been made to secure permission and provide appropriate credit for photographic material. The publisher deeply regrets any omission and pledges to correct errors called to its attention in subsequent editions. Unless otherwise acknowledged, all photographs are the property of Scott Foresman, a division of Pearson Education. Photo locators denoted as follows: Top (T), Center (C), Bottom (B), Left (L), Right (R) Background (Bkgd)
Opener: Big Sesh Studios; Title Page: ©DK Images; 2 ©Richard T. Nowitz/Corbis; 3 (TL) ©Scott W. Smith/Animals Animals/Earth Scenes, (BR) Colin Keates, Courtesy of the Natural History Museum, London/©DK Images; 6 Natural History Museum/©DK Images; 7 Natural History Museum /©DK Images; 8 (CC, B) ©DK Images; 9 (TR, B) ©DK Images; 10 ©DK Images; 11 Giuliano Fornari/©DK Images; 12 ©Francois Gohler/Photo Researchers, Inc.; 13 ©The Natural History Museum, London

ISBN: 0-328-13787-1

Fossils and Dinosaurs

by Jennifer Reynolds

Glossary

dinosaur	animals that lived on Earth long ago
extinct	no longer living on Earth
fossil	a print or part of a plant or animal from long ago
paleontologist	a scientist who studies fossils

How can we learn about the past?

Rocks can tell stories about the past.
Scientists called **paleontologists** look at rocks.
They use them to tell what plants and animals were like long ago.
These rocks may be fossils.

A paleontologist at work

Fossils can give us some clues about these plants and animals.
What questions do you have about life on Earth long ago?

Paleontologists learn different things from different fossils.
Paleontologists ask questions about life on Earth long ago.

A **fossil** is a print of a plant or animal from long ago.
Fossils can be footprints.
Fossils can be parts of plants or animals.
Some fossils are old bones.

Fossil of an animal footprint in the mud

Fossil of a leaf in the mud

How Fossils Form

This is a lizard fossil.
The lizard lived long ago.
The lizard died.
It got covered with sand and mud.

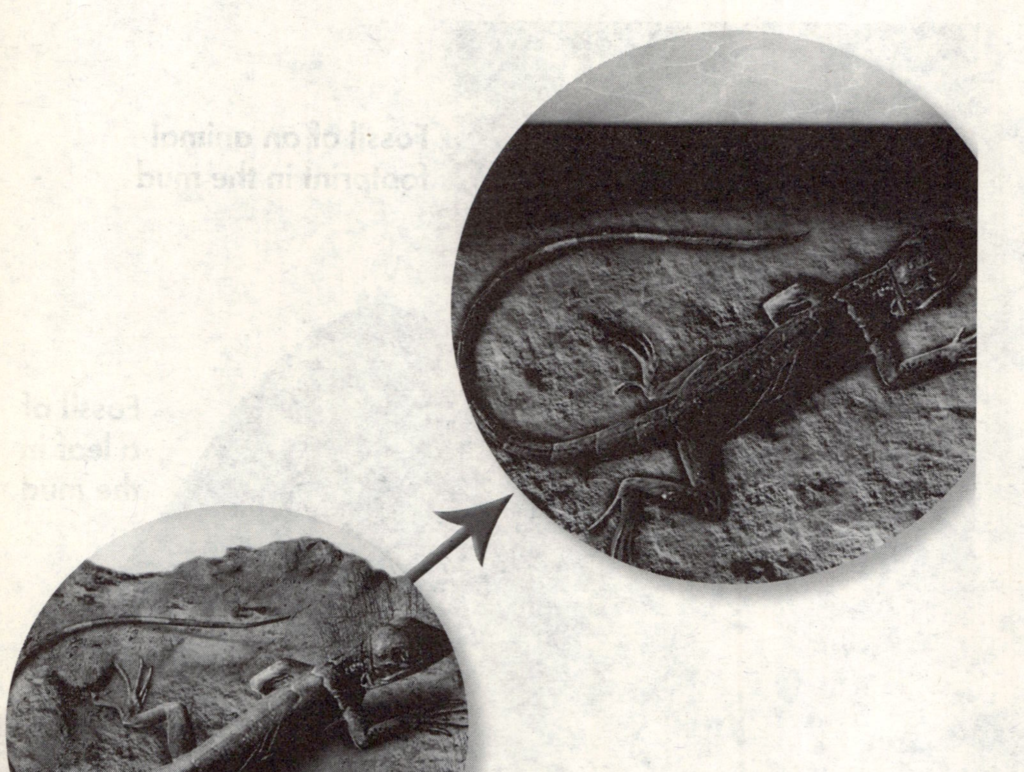

Then palentologists found another
Oviraptor fossil.
This Oviraptor fossil was sitting on the eggs.
Now paleontologists think the eggs were the
Oviraptor's own eggs.
They think the Oviraptor was keeping its
eggs safe.

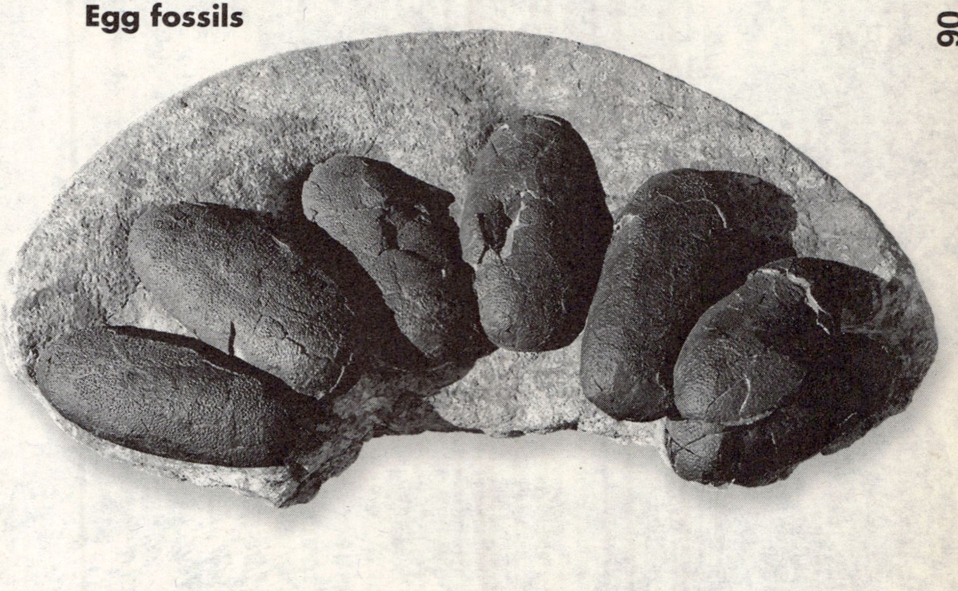

Egg fossils

What are some new discoveries?

Paleontologists found these fossils of eggs.
They also found a fossil of an Oviraptor near the eggs.
They thought the Oviraptor took the eggs to eat them.

Many years went by.
The sand and mud turned into rock.
The print of the lizard got left in the rock.
Now it is a fossil.

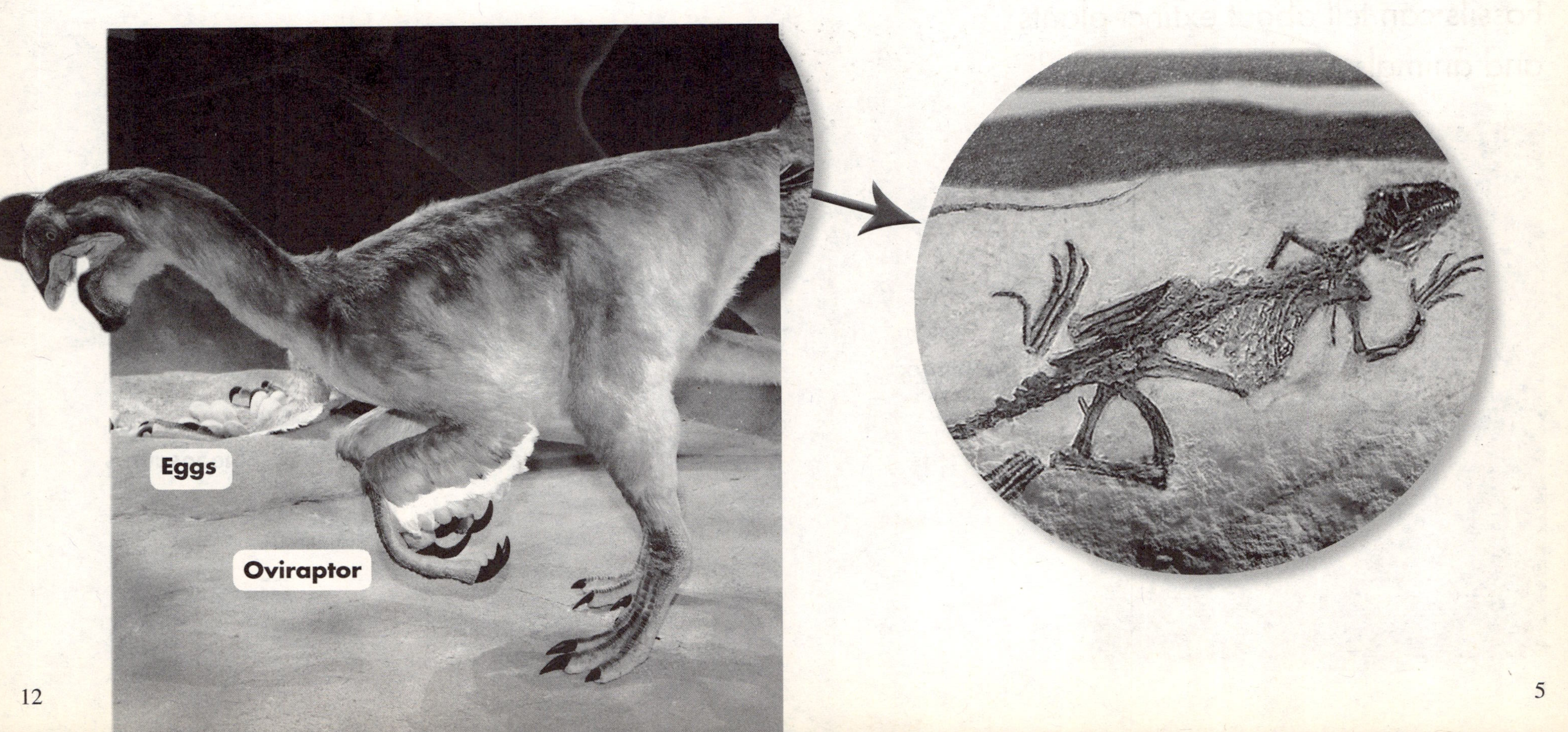

What can we learn from fossils?

Fossils tell about plants and animals
of the past.
Some plants and animals do not live on
Earth anymore.
They are **extinct.**
Fossils can tell about extinct plants
and animals.

Archaeopteryx
fossil

Fossils show that a Stegosaurus had
a large body.
It had a small head and a small mouth.
Paleontologists think this dinosaur ate plants.

Stegosaurus

Learning about Dinosaurs

Some dinosaur bones have turned
into fossils.
Paleontologists look at these fossils.
These fossils give clues about what dinosaurs
looked like.

Sometimes plants and animals stop getting
what they need.
Plants and animals die when this happens.
Plants and animals may become extinct
when habitats change.

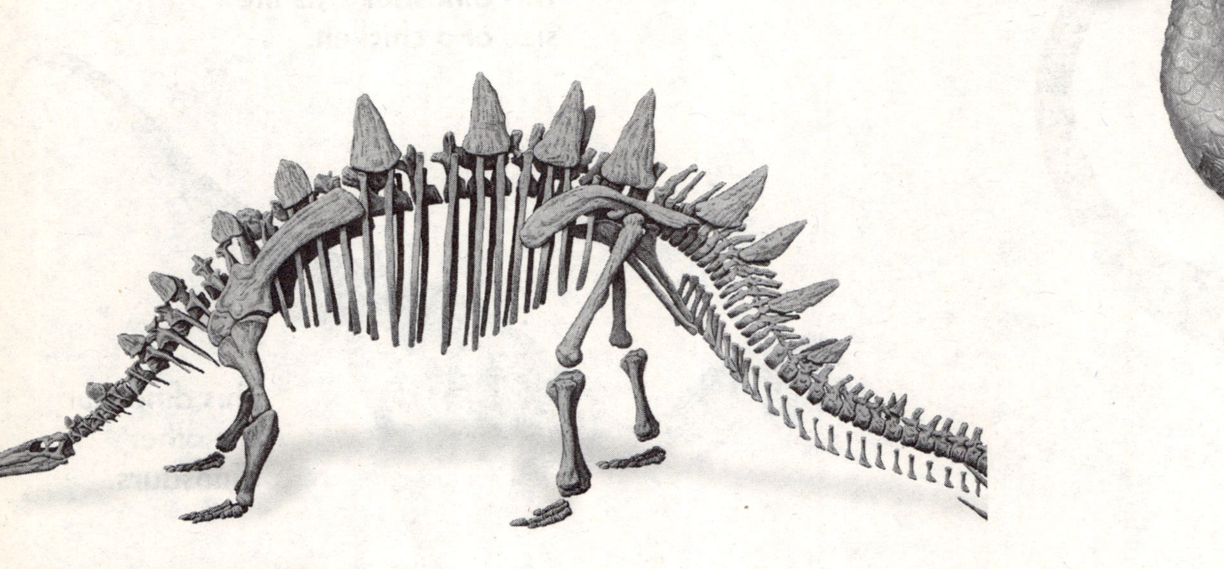

Stegosaurus skeleton

This Archaeopteryx
is now extinct.

What were dinosaurs like?

Dinosaurs were animals that lived
a long time ago.
Now dinosaurs are extinct.
They do not live on Earth anymore.

Some dinosaurs were big.
Some dinosaurs were small.
Some dinosaurs ate plants.
Some dinosaurs ate other animals.

Barosaurus
was very tall.

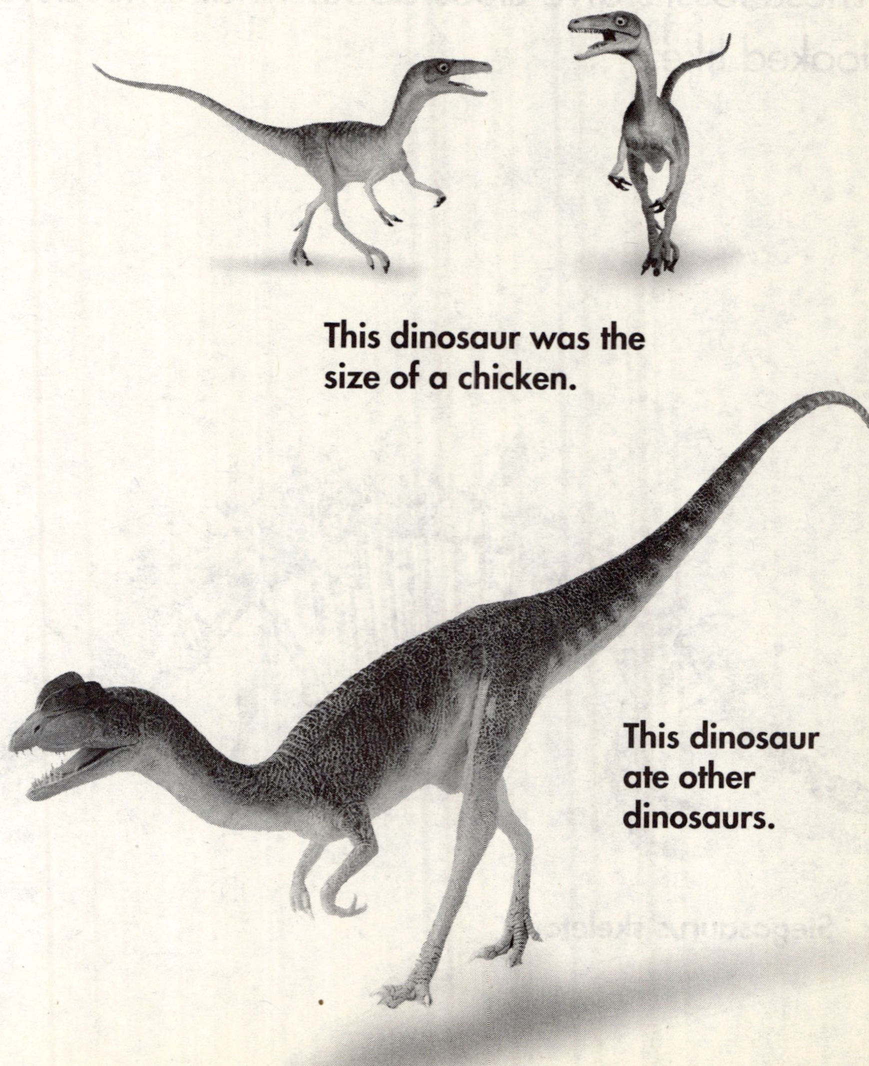

This dinosaur was the
size of a chicken.

This dinosaur
ate other
dinosaurs.

Properties of Matter

by Ann J. Jacobs

Genre	Comprehension Skill	Text Features	Science Content
Nonfiction	Draw Conclusions	• Captions • Call Outs • Labels • Glossary	Matter

Scott Foresman Science 2.8

PEARSON
Scott Foresman

ISBN 0-328-13790-1

90000

9 780328 137909

scottforesman.com

95

What did you learn?

1. What are the three states of matter?

2. What is one way solids are different from liquids and gases?

3. **Writing** in Science Heating can change matter. Write to explain how heating can change the state of matter. Use words from the book as you write.

4. **Draw Conclusions** You put a glass of ice cubes outside on a very hot day and returned later to find the glass had only water in it. What happened to cause the change?

Photographs: Every effort has been made to secure permission and provide appropriate credit for photographic material. The publisher deeply regrets any omission and pledges to correct errors called to its attention in subsequent editions. Unless otherwise acknowledged, all photographs are the property of Scott Foresman, a division of Pearson Education. Photo locators denoted as follows: Top (T), Center (C), Bottom (B), Left (L), Right (R) Background (Bkgd)
Opener: (CR) ©Photodisc Green/Getty Images, (Bkgd) ©Charles Gupton/Corbis; 2 Brand X Pictures, (CR) Getty Images; 16 Brand X Pictures; 21 ©Craig Tuttle/Corbis; 23 ©Nedra Westwater/Robert Harding Picture Library Ltd.

ISBN: 0-328-13790-1

Copyright © Pearson Education, Inc.

All Rights Reserved. Printed in the United States of America. The blackline masters in this publication are designed for use with appropriate equipment to reproduce copies for classroom use only. Scott Foresman grants permission to classroom teachers to reproduce from these masters.

2 3 4 5 6 7 8 9 10 V004 13 12 11 10 09 08 07 06 05

Properties of Matter

by Ann J. Jacobs

Glossary

gas	matter that has mass and can change size and shape
liquid	matter that takes up space and has mass, but does not have its own shape
mass	the amount of matter in an object
mixture	something made up of two or more things that do not change
property	something about an object that you can find out with your senses
solid	matter that has its own mass, shape, and size
states of matter	solids, liquids, and gases

What is matter?

Everything is made of matter.
Matter is anything that takes up space
and has mass.

Mass is how much matter is in something.
All things made of matter have mass.
Everything you see is made of matter.

Heat can change other matter from
solids to liquids.
Wax melts when you burn a candle.

Look at the matter around you.
What will stay the same?
What can change?

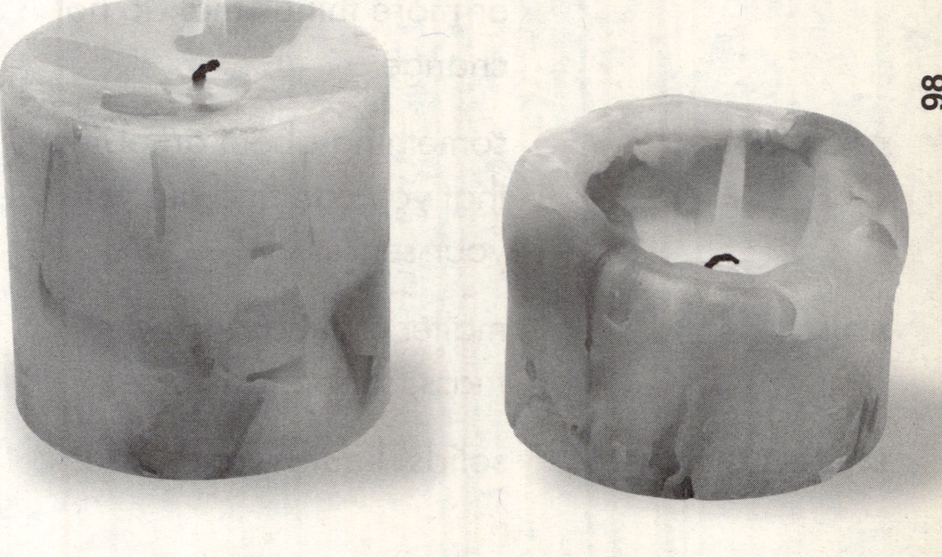

Heating Matter

Heating can change the state of matter.
Heat can change solids to liquids.
Heat can change liquids to gases.

Ice and snow melt when it is warm.
Solid water changes to a liquid.

Heat from the Sun makes water evaporate.

Matter is made of small parts.
A hand lens helps you see small parts
up close.
Some things you cannot see are made
of matter.
Air has matter!

Properties of Matter

Different kinds of matter have different properties.
A **property** is something you can observe about an object.

Color is a property of matter.
Shape is a property of matter.
Size is a property of matter too.

What colors are the pipe cleaners? Are they big or small?

The water will change to ice.
Ice is solid water.

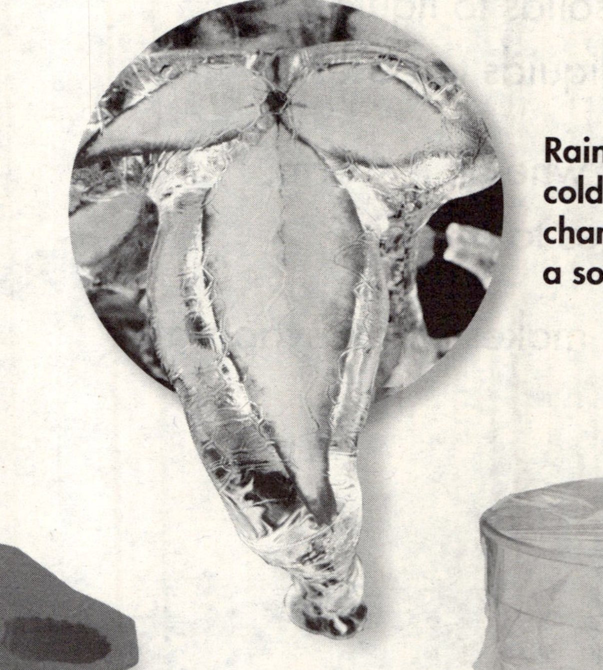

Rain will freeze when it is cold. Water on the leaves changed from a liquid to a solid.

Water as a gas is water vapor. It changes to a liquid when it meets a cold glass. See the water drops.

How can cooling and heating change matter?

Water is matter.
Water can change.
Water will freeze when it is very cold.

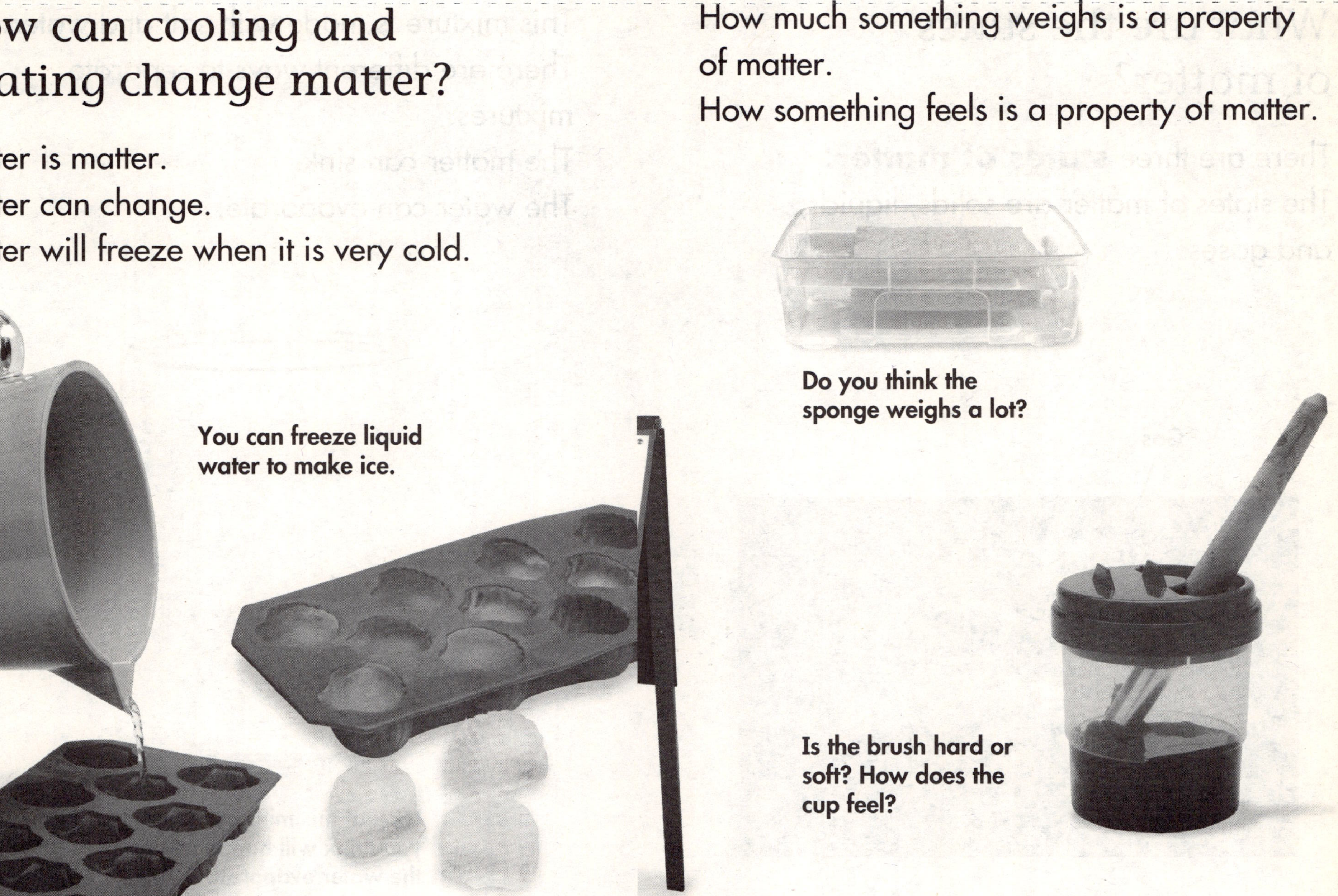

You can freeze liquid
water to make ice.

How much something weighs is a property
of matter.

How something feels is a property of matter.

Do you think the
sponge weighs a lot?

Is the brush hard or
soft? How does the
cup feel?

What are the states of matter?

There are three **states of matter.**
The states of matter are solids, liquids, and gases.

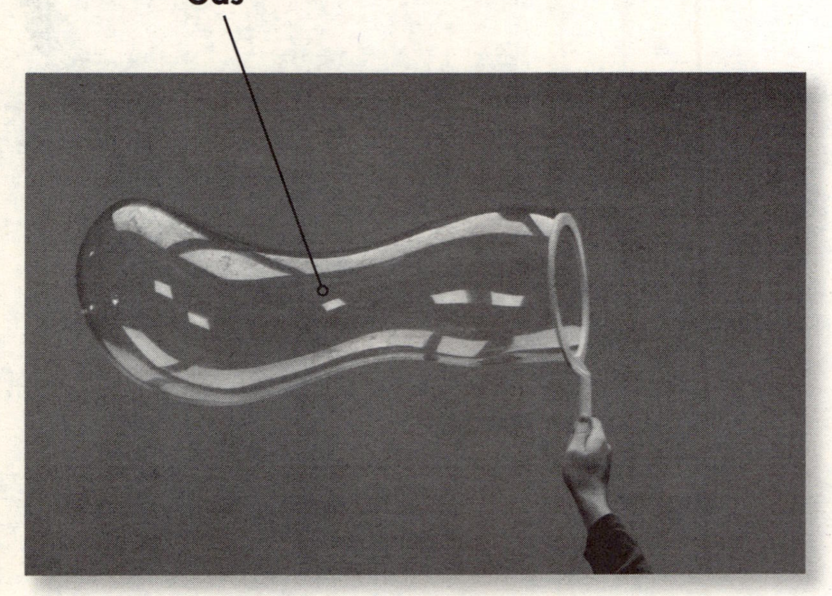

This mixture is made with salt and water.
There are different ways to separate mixtures.
The matter can sink.
The water can evaporate.

Look at this mixture. What do you think will happen when the water evaporates?

Mixing with Water

Some mixtures are made with water.
This mixture is made with sand and water.

Look at this mixture.
You can see the
sand and the water.

A **solid** is matter that has its own size
and shape.
Solids take up space.
Solids have mass.

Use a ruler to find out
how long, wide, and
tall solids are.

You can use a
balance to find the
mass of a solid.

This is a mixture of fruits.
You can see each part.
You can separate a mixture.
The parts stay the same.

Mixing and Separating Matter

You can put different kinds of matter together.
This makes a mixture.

A **mixture** is made up of two or more things.
These things do not change.

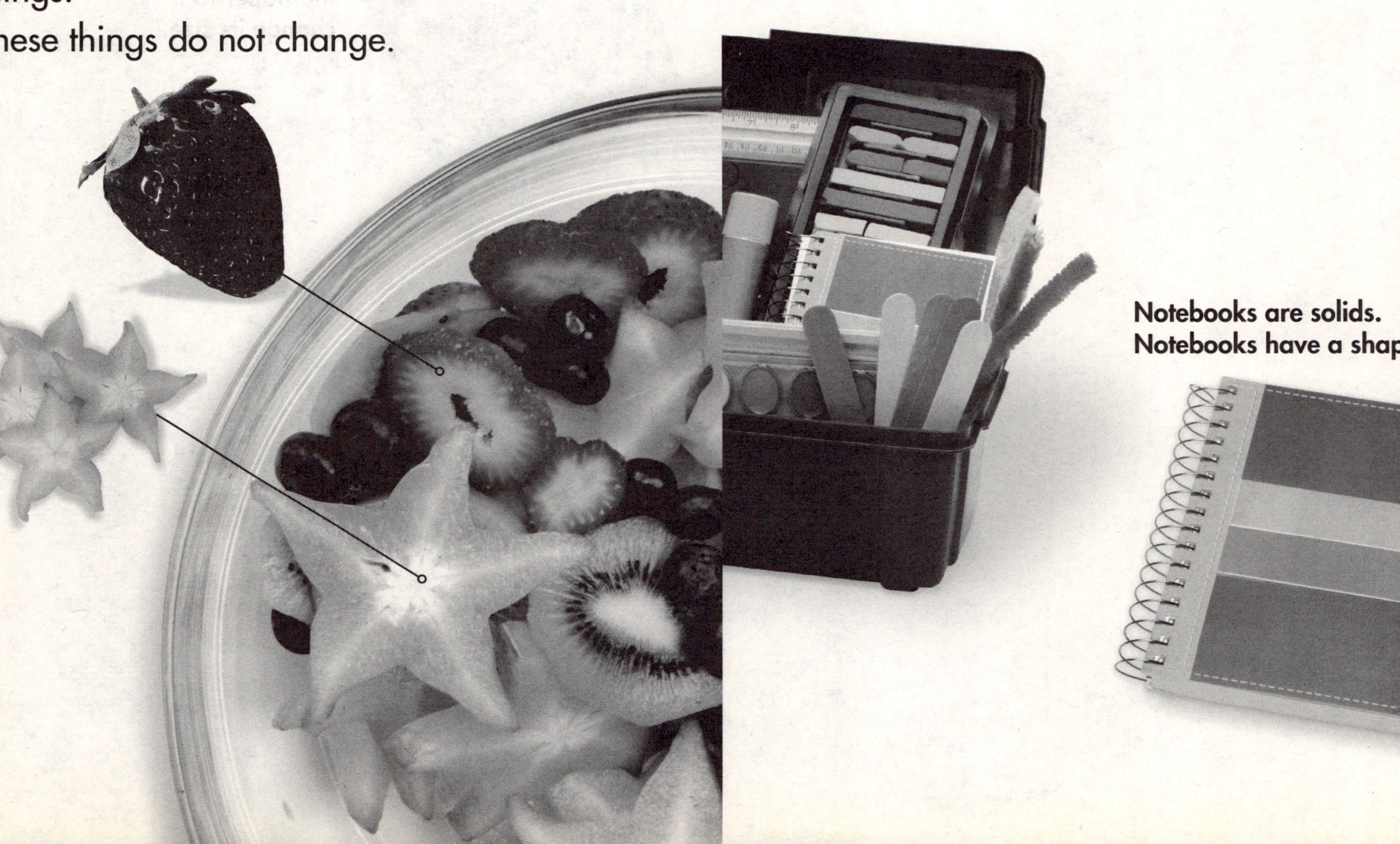

Liquids

Liquid is matter that does not have its
own shape.
Liquids take the shape of what they are in.
Liquids take up space and have mass.

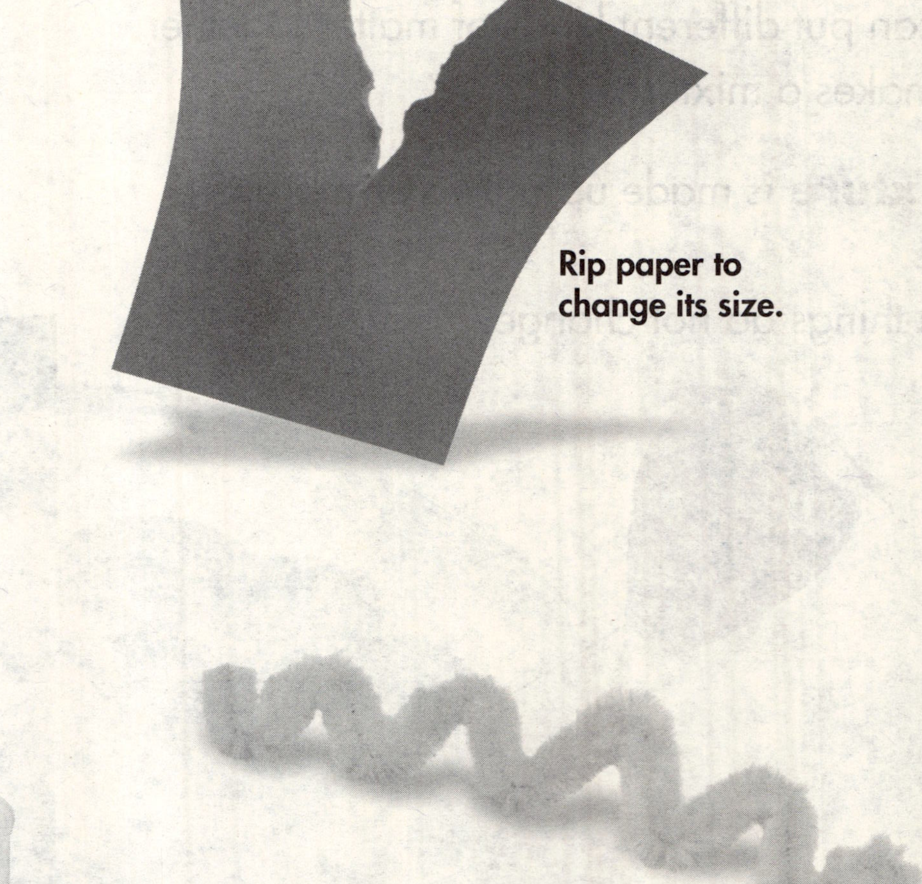

How can matter be changed?

Matter can be changed in many ways.
You can change the size of matter.
You can change the shape of matter.

**Fold paper into
a new shape.**

**Press clay into
a new shape.**

Water is a liquid.
Put water in a jar.
The water will take the shape of the jar.

**Liquids can be measured.
Use a cup such as this one.
Volume is the amount of
space a liquid takes up.**

Gases

Gas does not have its own shape.
Gas is matter that takes the size and
shape of what it is in.
Gas takes up all the space inside what
it is in.

Gas can change size and shape.
Gas has mass.
You breathe air.
Air is made of gases.

Energy

by Arlene Block

Genre	Comprehension Skill	Text Features	Science Content
Nonfiction	Infer	• Captions • Call Outs • Labels • Glossary	Energy

Scott Foresman Science 2.9

PEARSON
Scott Foresman

ISBN 0-328-13793-6

9 780328 137930

90000

scottforesman.com

What did you learn?

1. Where does Earth get energy?

2. What are some ways people use energy?

3. **Writing** in Science There are different types of energy. Write to tell about two types you read about. Use words from the book as you write.

4. **Infer** It is a hot and sunny day. One person wears a light shirt. One person wears a dark shirt. Which person will stay cooler? Why?

Photographs: Every effort has been made to secure permission and provide appropriate credit for photographic material. The publisher deeply regrets any omission and pledges to correct errors called to its attention in subsequent editions. Unless otherwise acknowledged, all photographs are the property of Scott Foresman, a division of Pearson Education. Photo locators denoted as follows: Top (T), Center (C), Bottom (B), Left (L), Right (R) Background (Bkgd)
Opener: ©Kelly-Mooney Photography/Corbis; 1 ©Steven Gorton and Gary Ombler/©DK Images; 2 ©Jim Cummins/Corbis; 3 Getty Images; 4 ©Roger Ressmeyer/Skylab/NRL/NASA/Corbis; 5 ©Photodisc Green/Getty Images; 6 Corbis; 7 ©John Conrad/Corbis; 8 ©Laureen March/Corbis; 9 ©Jon Feingersh/Corbis; 13 ©Tom Stewart/Corbis; 16 Hemera Technologies; 17 ©Royalty-Free/Corbis; 18 ©Craig Tuttle/Corbis, ©Lonny Kalfus/Getty Images; 19 ©DK Images; 21 ©Randy Lincks/Corbis, ©Tony Freeman/PhotoEdit; 22©Steven Gorton and Gary Ombler/©DK Images; 23 ©Jon Feingersh/Corbis

ISBN: 0-328-13793-6

by Arlene Block

Glossary

conductor   something that lets heat easily move through it

energy   anything that can do work or make a change

fuel   something that is burned to make heat

reflect   light hits something and bounces back

shadow   something made when light is blocked

solar energy   light and heat from the Sun

source   a place from which something comes

111

What is energy?

You use energy all the time.
Things that can do work and cause change
have **energy.**
You use energy when you walk.
You use energy when you breathe.
You use energy while you sleep.

There are many kinds of energy.
How do you know what has or uses energy?
Is it doing work?
Can it change something?
Then it has energy!

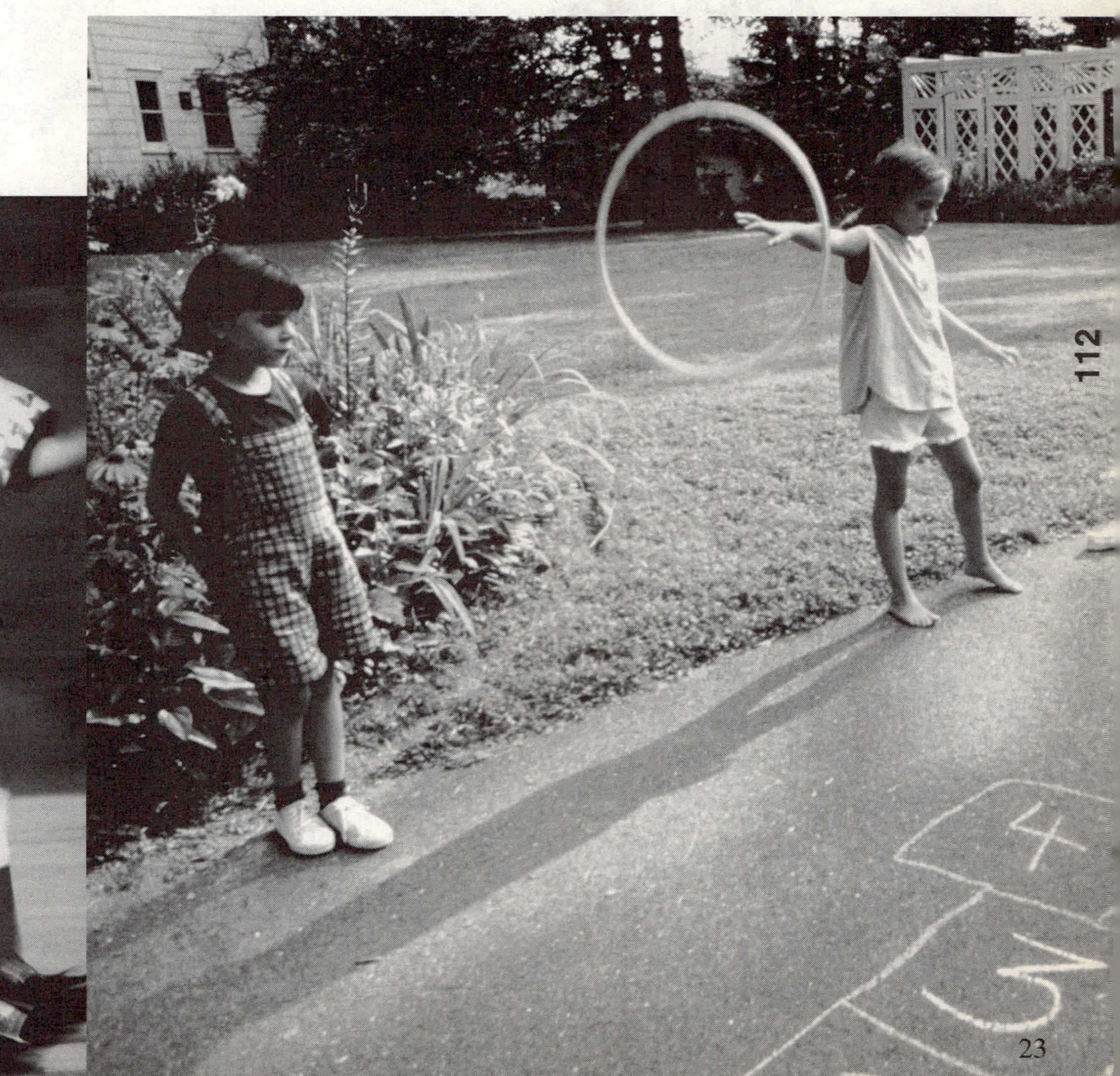

Using Electricity Safely

Turn on a light.
Electricity makes the light work.
Electricity makes this clock work.

Do not use electricity near water.
Do not pull on cords.
Do not touch wires.
How else can you use electricity in
a safe way?

Electricity can
be stored in
batteries.

What has energy?
Can it do work?
Can it make something change?
Then it has energy.

Energy from the Sun

Earth gets energy from the Sun.
The Sun gives Earth heat.
Heat and light from the Sun are
solar energy.

Light from the Sun helps people and
animals see.
Earth would be dark without the Sun.

The Sun

Wind is a kind of energy.
Wind energy can move the boat.

Sound is a kind of energy too.

Wind energy

Sound energy

What are other kinds of energy?

You use different kinds of energy.
How can you make this grocery cart move?
You can push it.
Then it will have energy of motion.

People can use solar energy.
Solar energy heats this home.

How do living things use energy?

Most living things need energy from the Sun.
Plants use green leaves to make food.
Plants use sunlight to make food.
Plants use water and air too.

Plants need food to live and grow.

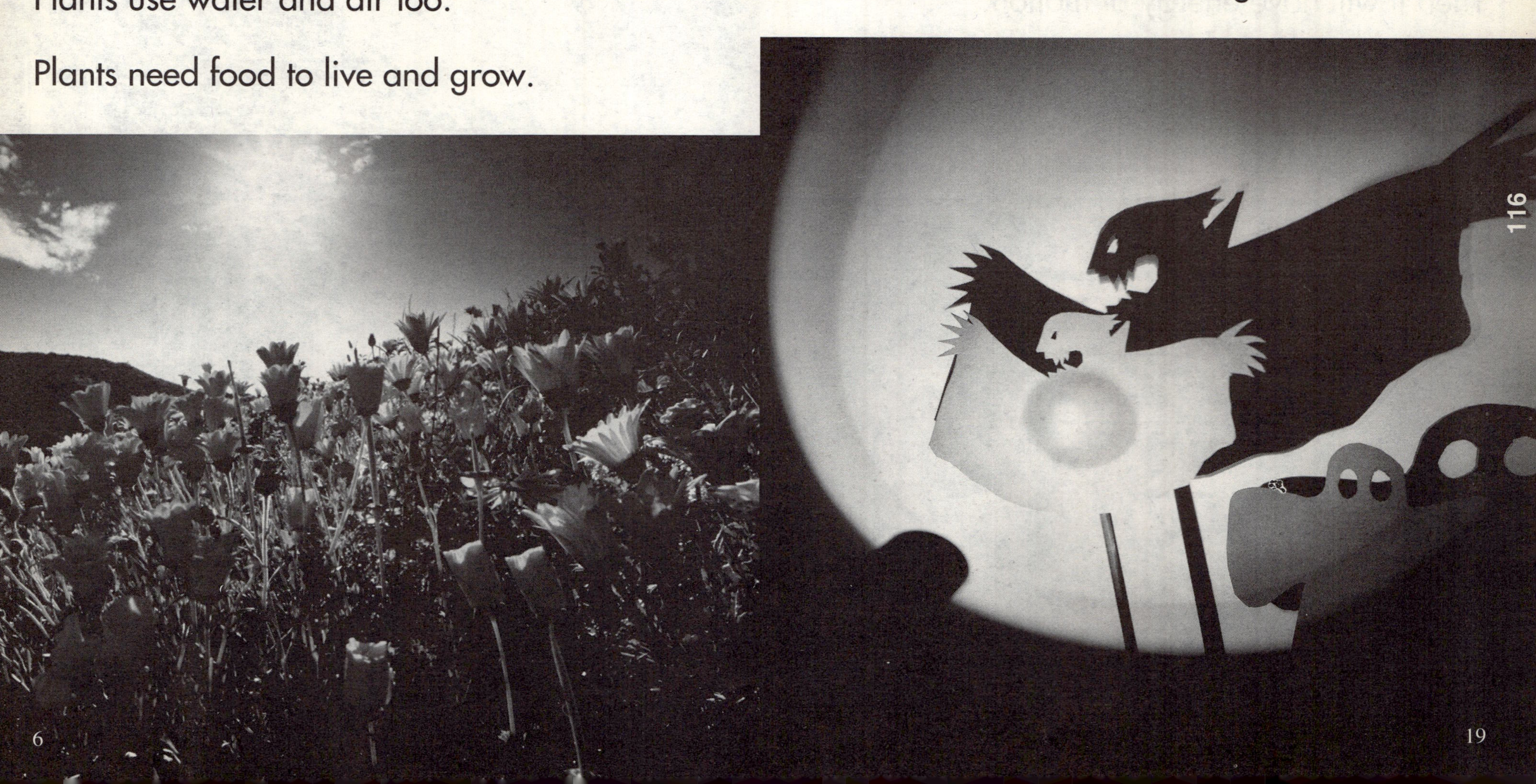

Use a flashlight to make a shadow.
Cut a shape from paper.
Use it to block the light.

Move the shape close to the light.
Move the shape far from the light.
How does the shadow change?

Shadows

A **shadow** is made when light is blocked.
Go out in the sunlight.
Your body blocks the light.
You make a shadow.

Shadows change during the day.
Shadows change when the Sun looks high
and low in the sky.

Animals use energy to move.
Animals get energy from food.
Animals use energy to live and grow.

Some animals eat plants.
Some animals eat animals that eat plants.
The plants get energy from the Sun.

How People Get Energy

People get energy from food.
Food gives people energy to grow.
Food gives people energy to move.

We see mostly white light.
Many colors make up white light.
You can see the colors in a rainbow.

Dark colors take in light.
Light colors reflect light.
Wear light colors to stay cool.

Food gives you energy to play.
Food gives you energy to work.

How does light move?

Light is a kind of energy.
The Sun is one source of light.
Fire and flashlights are other sources of light.
Most light sources give off heat too.

Light moves in a straight line.
Light can move through some things.
Light **reflects** when it hits something.
It reflects when it bounces back.

This shows how light reflects.

Here are five food groups.
Eat foods from each group every day.
These foods can help you grow.
They can help you stay healthy.

Milk, yogurt, cheese

Vegetables

The pan is made of metal.
Metal is a conductor.
A **conductor** lets heat move through it.

Cloth is not a good conductor.
The mitt is made of cloth.
It keeps heat from moving to your hand.

Heat does not go through the mitt to your hand.

How Heat Moves

Heat starts at a warm place.
It moves to a cooler place.
The burner is hot.
The pan and food are cold.
Heat moves from the burner to the pan.
Then heat moves from the pan to the food.

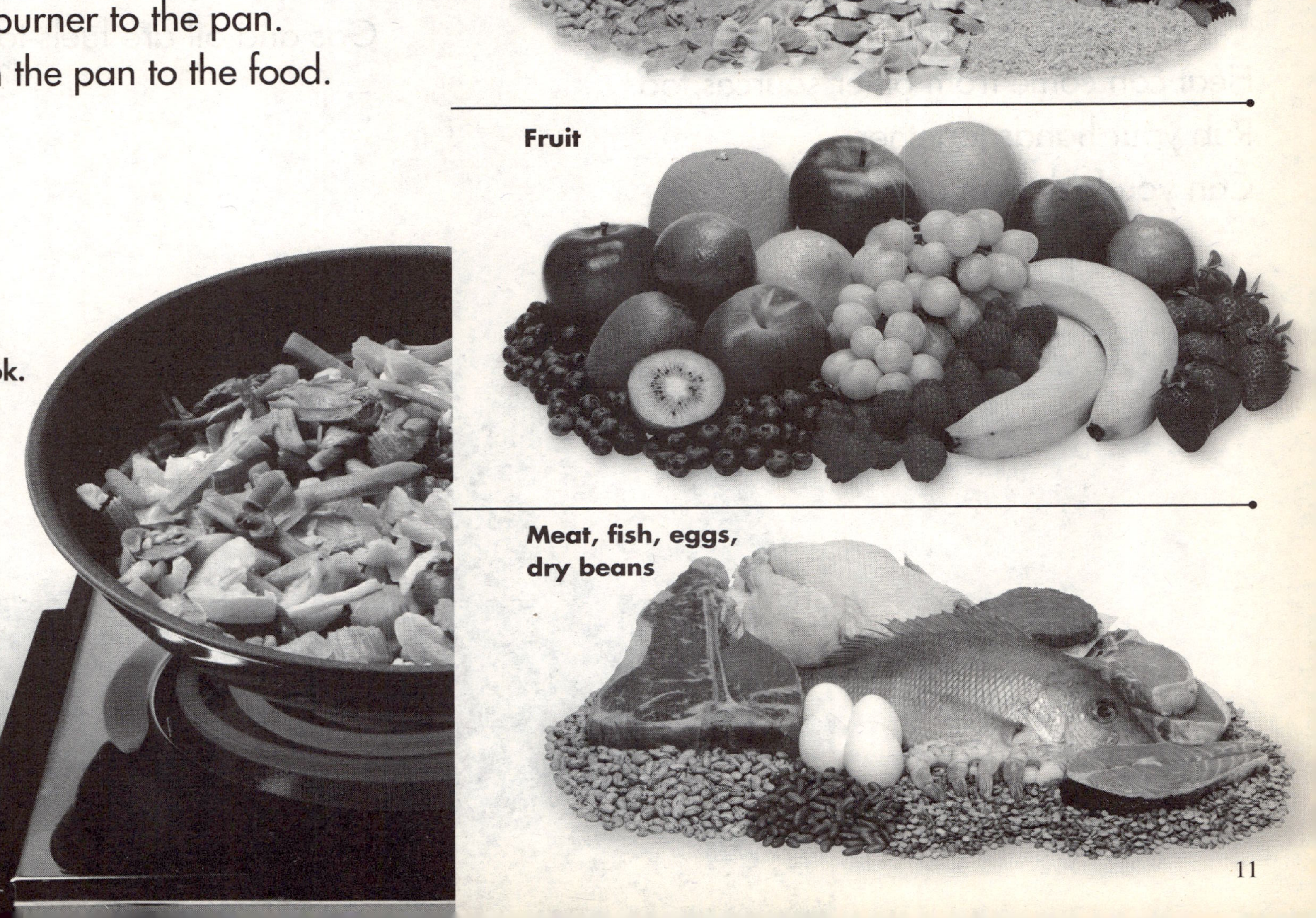

People use
heat to cook.

What are some sources of heat?

Sunlight is a source of heat.
A **source** is where something comes from.
Heat comes from sunlight.

Heat can come from other sources too.
Rub your hands together.
Can you feel them get warm?

Fire is a source of heat.
Wood burns to make fire.
Wood is a fuel.

Fuel is burned to make heat.
Coal is another kind of fuel.
Gas and oil are fuels too.

Science

Science

Forces and Motion

by Arlene Block

123

Genre	Comprehension Skill	Text Features	Science Content
Nonfiction	Put Things In Order	• Labels • Glossary	Forces and Motion

Scott Foresman Science 2.10

ISBN 0-328-13796-0

PEARSON

Scott Foresman

scottforesman.com

Vocabulary

attract

force

friction

gravity

motion

repel

simple machine

work

What did you learn?

1. How can you make objects move?

2. What is gravity?

3. **Writing** in Science You can change how things move. Write to tell about some things you can do. Use words from the book as you write.

4. **Put Things In Order** How could you make a magnet attract and then repel another magnet? Tell, in order, what you would do.

Photographs: Every effort has been made to secure permission and provide appropriate credit for photographic material. The publisher deeply regrets any omission and pledges to correct errors called to its attention in subsequent editions. Unless otherwise acknowledged, all photographs are the property of Scott Foresman, a division of Pearson Education. Photo locators denoted as follows: Top (T), Center (C), Bottom (B), Left (L), Right (R) Background (Bkgd)
Opener: (Bkgd) ©Lester Letkowitz/Corbis, (TR) ©Photographer's Choice/Getty Images, (Bkgd) NASA Image Exchange; Title Page: ©Taxi/Getty Images; 2 ©First Light/Corbis; 3 ©Joyce Choo/Corbis; 4 (BR) ©Stone/Getty Images, (TR) ©Chris Carroll/Corbis; 6 ©Wally McNamee/Corbis; 7 ©Stone/Getty Images; 9 ©Chapman/NewSport/Corbis; 10 (T) ©Mike Brinson/Getty Images, (B) ©Thinkstock/Superstock; 11 ©Taxi/Getty Images; 12 Getty Images; 13 ©Juergen & Christine Sohns/Animals Animals/ Earth Scenes

ISBN: 0-328-13796-0

Forces and Motion

by Arlene Block

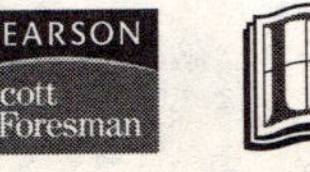

Glossary

attract	to pull toward something
force	a push or a pull
friction	a force that makes moving objects slow down or stop
gravity	a force that pulls things down to Earth
motion	the act of moving
repel	to push away
simple machine	a tool with few or no moving parts
work	what happens when a force makes an object move

How do objects move?

Motion is the act of moving.
Objects can move in different ways.

This swing moves back and forth.
A merry-go-round moves in a circle.

What a Magnet Can Attract

Magnets attract some metal objects.
Iron and copper are two metals.
Some nails are made of iron.
A magnet will attract a nail.
A penny is made of copper.
A magnet will not attract a penny.

Try using a magnet. See how it works!

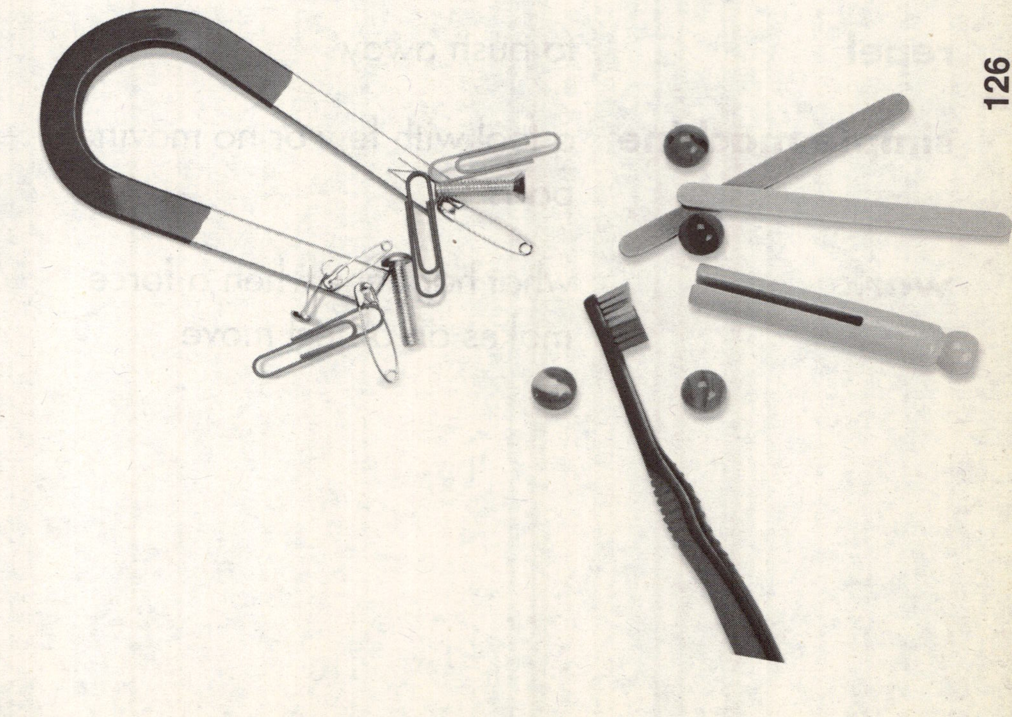

What are magnets?

Magnets **attract** some metal objects.
Attract means to pull toward.
Magnets **repel** other magnets.
Repel means to push away.

The ends of magnets are called poles.
Magnets have north and south poles.

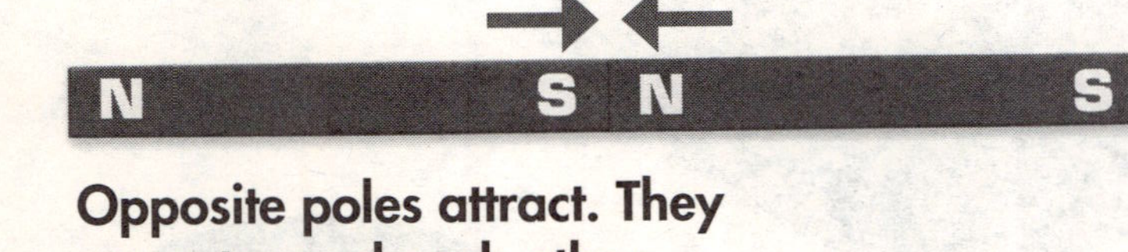

Opposite poles attract. They
move toward each other.

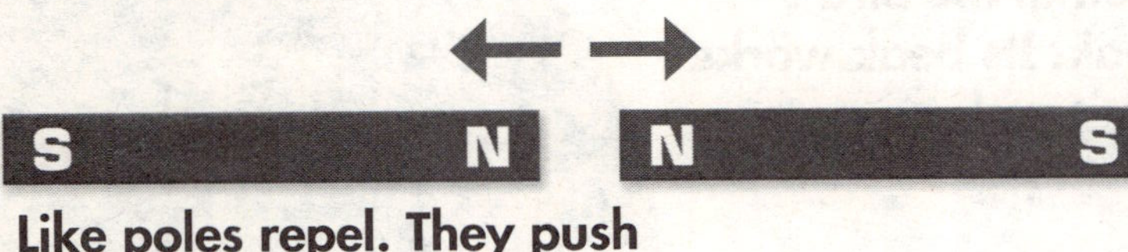

Like poles repel. They push
away from each other.

Force

How can you make objects move?
You can push or pull them.
A push or pull is a **force.**
A force changes the way objects move.

Use more force!
The object will move faster.

Gravity

Throw leaves in the air.
They fall down.
Gravity pulls the leaves down.
Gravity is a force.
Gravity pulls things down to Earth.

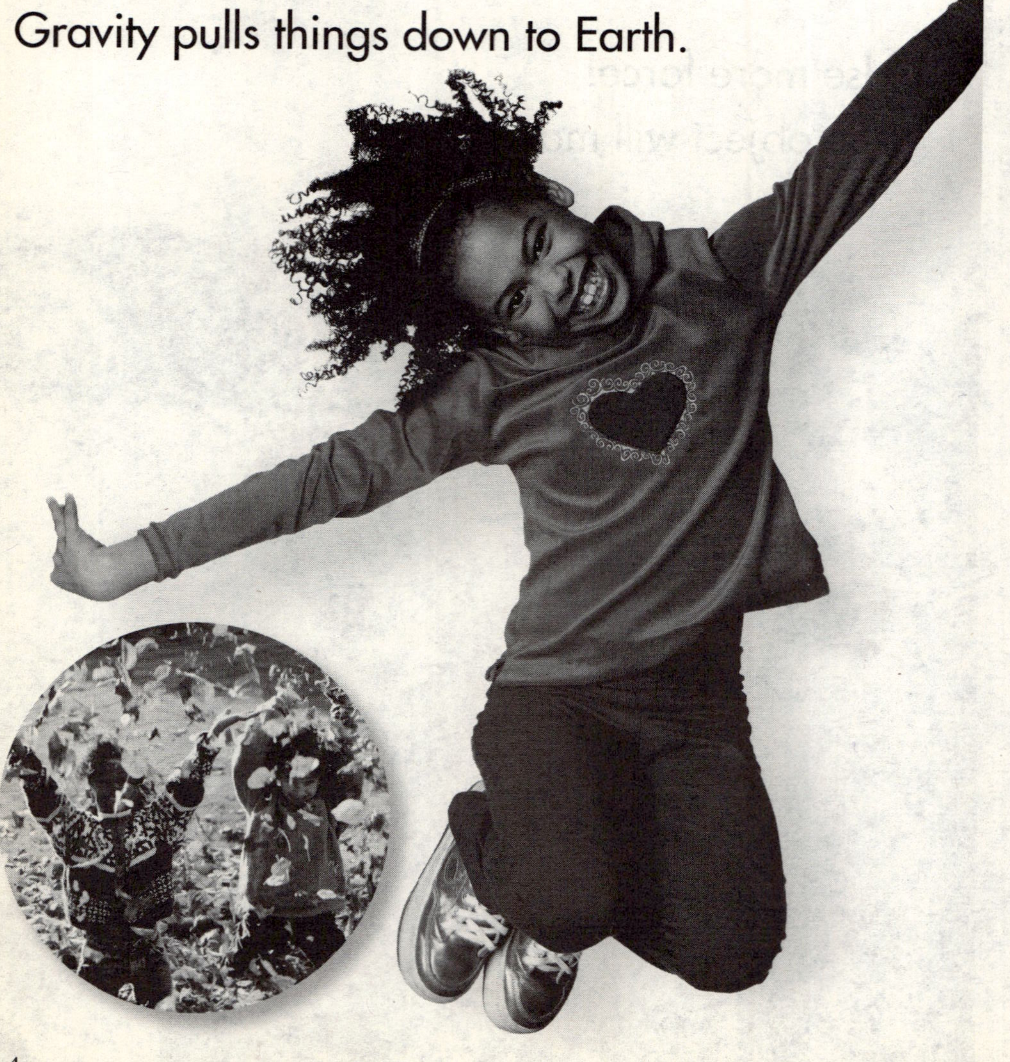

Animal Body Parts

Some animal body parts are like
simple machines.
Animals use them to do work.

Look at the bird's
beak. Its beak works
like two levers.

Look at this badger's claws.
It uses them like a wedge.

How can simple machines help you do work?

A **simple machine** is a tool.
A simple machine has few or no moving parts.
It can help you do work.
It can help you move things.

These are simple machines.

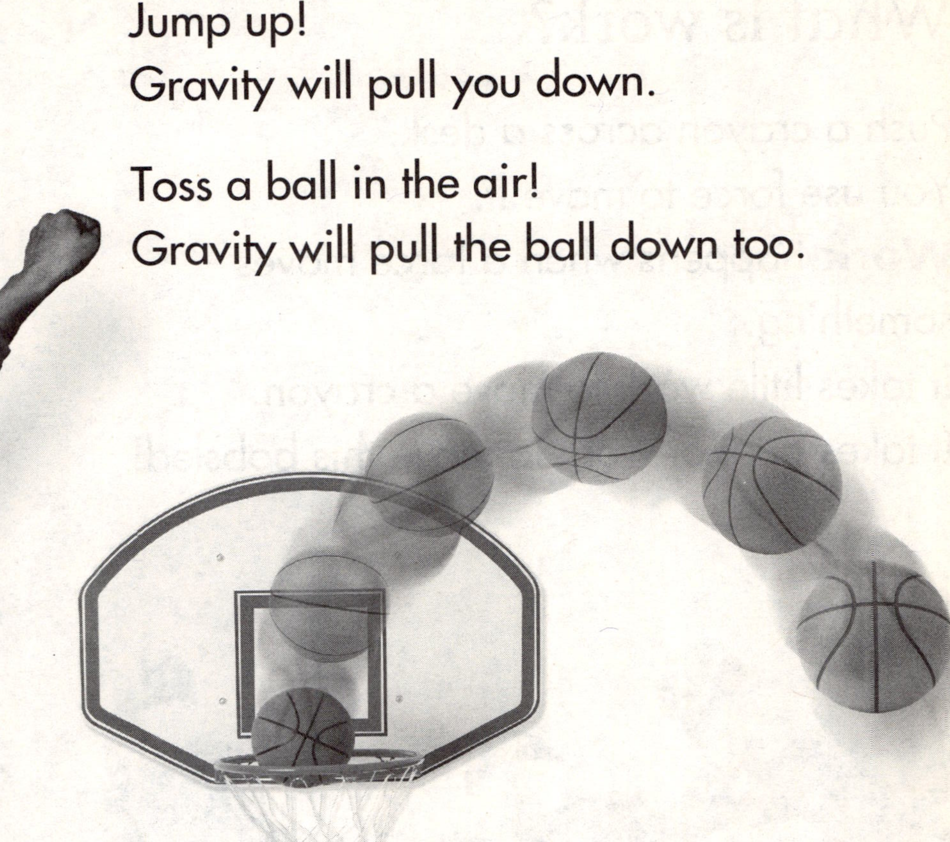

Jump up!
Gravity will pull you down.

Toss a ball in the air!
Gravity will pull the ball down too.

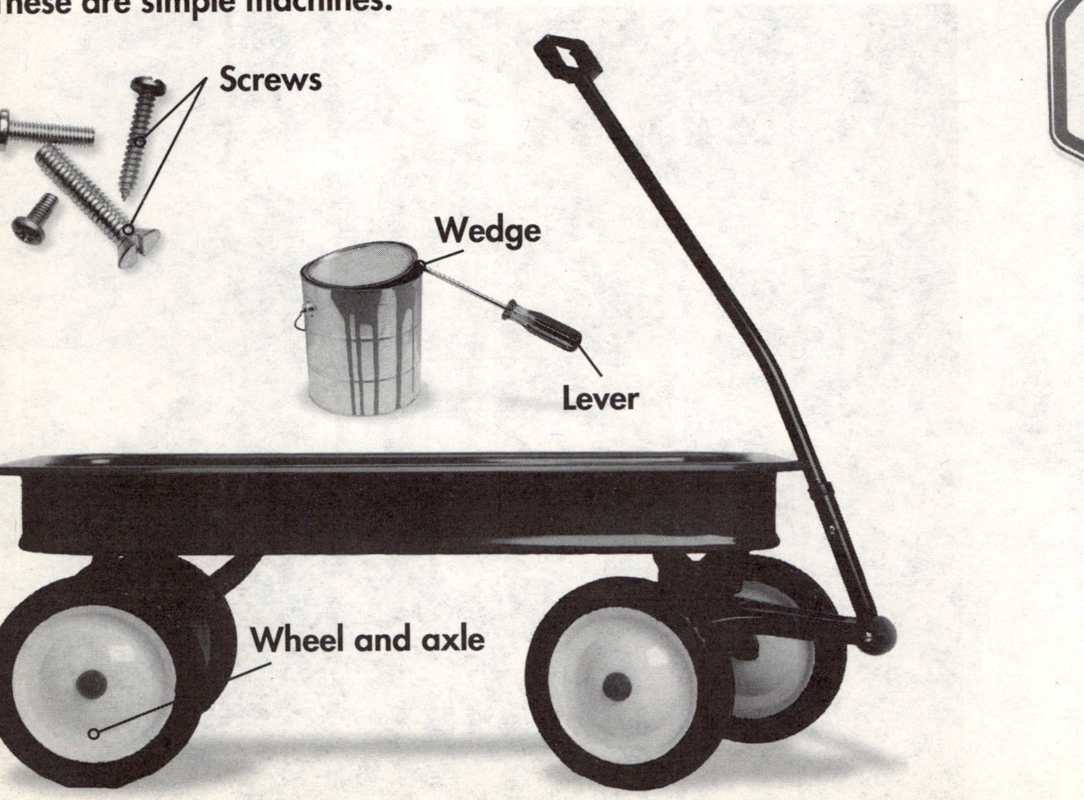

What is work?

Push a crayon across a desk.
You use force to move it.
Work happens when a force moves
something.
It takes little work to move a crayon.
It takes a lot of work to move this bobsled!

This bike moves on the grass.
The bike moves slowly.
The tires rub against the grass.
Friction makes the bike slow down.

Friction

Friction is a force.
Friction makes things move slowly.
Friction makes things stop.

This bike moves on the smooth road.
The bike moves fast.

When an object does not move, work
does not happen.
Look at the picture.
The people cannot make the rock move.
They are not doing work.

How can you change the way things move?

You can change how things move.
Use more or less force.

Tap a ball.
It will not move far.

Use more force.
Kick the ball hard.
It will go far!

Sound

by Ann J. Jacobs

Genre	Comprehension Skill	Text Features	Science Content
Nonfiction	Important Details	• Labels • Glossary	Sound

Scott Foresman Science 2.11

PEARSON

Scott Foresman

scottforesman.com

What did you learn?

1. How is sound made?

2. What is pitch?

3. **Writing** in Science Sound moves through gases, liquids, and solids. In your own words write to give an example of each. Use words from the book as you write.

4. **Important Details** Crickets make sound. What are some important details about how they do this?

Illustration: 23 Philip Williams
Photographs: Every effort has been made to secure permission and provide appropriate credit for photographic material. The publisher deeply regrets any omission and pledges to correct errors called to its attention in subsequent editions. Unless otherwise acknowledged, all photographs are the property of Scott Foresman, a division of Pearson Education. Photo locators denoted as follows: Top (T), Center (C), Bottom (B), Left (L), Right (R) Background (Bkgd)
Title Page: ©DK Images; 2 ©Thinkstock; 3 ©Thinkstock; 4 (T) ©Martin Harvey/NHPA Limited, (B) ©Jeff Hunter/Getty Images; 5 (CC) ©George Hall/Corbis, (B) ©Walter Hodges/Corbis; 6 (T) ©The Image Bank/Getty Images, (B) ©Photodisc Green/Getty Images; 7 (T, B)©Royalty-Free/Corbis; 8 ©Tom & Dee Ann McCarthy/Corbis; 12 ©DK Images; 14 ©Taxi/Getty Images; 15 ©Mark Boulton/Photo Researchers, Inc.; 16 Digital Vision; 17 ©Roger Wilmshurts/Frank Lane Picture Agency/Corbis; 19 ©Jeffrey L. Rotman/ Corbis; 20 (BL) ©Stephen Dalton/NHPA Limited, (R) ©DK Images, (CL) ©Stockbyte; 21 (TL) ©Royalty Free/Corbis, (TC) ©Image Quest 3-D/NHPA Limited, (BC) Corbis, (BR) ©Brownie Harris/Corbis

ISBN: 0-328-13799-5

Glossary

loudness how loud or soft a sound is

pitch how high or low a sound is

vibrate to move quickly back and forth

Sound

by Ann J. Jacobs

What is sound?

Look at the band.
You can see lots of instruments.
Each one makes a sound when it is played.

What are some sounds around you?

There are sounds all around.
You might hear a fire truck.
You might hear children.
You might hear a fly.

Every day we hear sounds.
Just listen!

Sound is made when something vibrates.
Vibrate means to move quickly back and forth.
This flute makes the air vibrate, which makes sound.

Loudness

You can use loudness to tell about a sound.
Loudness is how loud or soft a sound is.

A rattlesnake shakes its tail.
Its tail works like maracas.

A lobster makes sounds.
It rubs its antenna on the side of its head.
Its antenna works like a violin.

21

How do some animals make sounds?

Animals make sounds in lots of ways.
A cricket uses its wings.
It rubs them together.
The wings vibrate and make a sound.
The sound is like running your fingers
on the teeth of a comb.

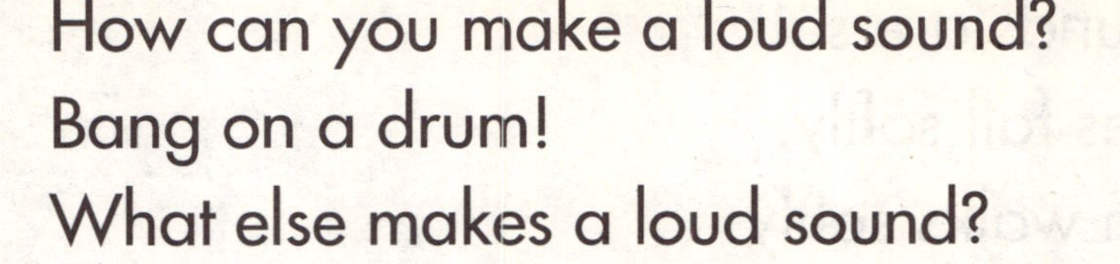

How can you make a loud sound?
Bang on a drum!
What else makes a loud sound?

Some sounds are soft.
The leaves fall softly.
The kitten walks softly.

Sound moves faster through water than
through air.
Sound moves the fastest through solids,
such as wood.

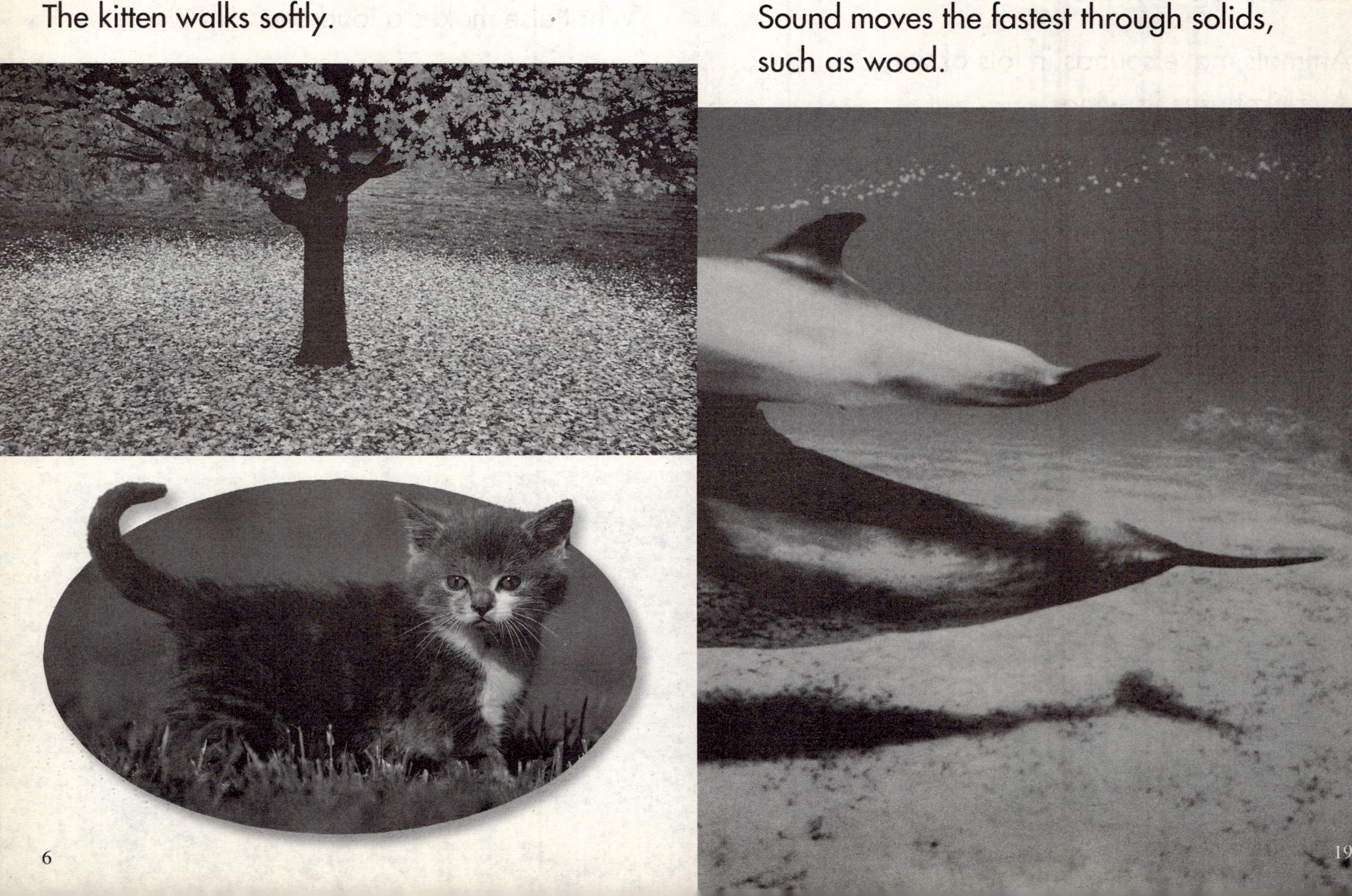

This dolphin clicks.
The sound moves through the water.

Tap a drum lightly.
It makes a soft sound.
What else makes soft sounds?

What is pitch?

Pitch means how high or low a sound is.
Things that vibrate fast have a high pitch.
Things that vibrate slowly have a low pitch.

This bird pecks at a tree.
The sound moves through the tree and the air.

142

How does sound travel?

Sound goes through solids, liquids,
and gases.
Sound moves fast through the air.

This lion lets out a roar.
The sound goes through the air.

Do you think this violin has a low or
high pitch?
It can have a high pitch when the strings
vibrate fast.
It can have a lower pitch when the strings
vibrate slowly.

Find out more about pitch.
Blow across the top of a bottle.
What happens to the air inside the bottle?

The bullfrog makes sounds with a low pitch.
This bird makes sounds with a high pitch.

Lots of air,
low pitch

Animals make many kinds of sounds.
Animal sounds can have a low or a
high pitch.

The air inside the bottle vibrates.
Bottles with a lot of air make a sound with
a low pitch.
Bottles with less air make a sound with
a high pitch.

Look at the bottles.
Which one makes the sound with the
highest pitch?

Which one makes the sound with the
lowest pitch?

Earth and Space

by Harriet Stansbury

147

Genre	Comprehension Skill	Text Features	Science Content
Nonfiction	Alike and Different	• Captions • Labels • Glossary	Earth and Space

Scott Foresman Science 2.12

PEARSON

Scott Foresman

DK

scottforesman.com

ISBN 0-328-13802-9

90000

9 780328 138029

Vocabulary

axis

constellation

crater

orbit

phase

rotation

solar system

What did you learn?

1. What is the Sun made of?

2. What is Earth's axis?

3. **Writing** in Science Earth's rotation causes night and day. Write to explain how this happens.

4. **Alike and Different** Look at the picture of the planets in our solar system. How are the planets alike? How are they different?

Illustrations: 6, 8, 15, 21, 22 Bob Kayganich
Photographs: Every effort has been made to secure permission and provide appropriate credit for photographic material. The publisher deeply regrets any omission and pledges to correct errors called to its attention in subsequent editions. Unless otherwise acknowledged, all photographs are the property of Scott Foresman, a division of Pearson Education. Photo locators denoted as follows: Top (T), Center (C), Bottom (B), Left (L), Right (R) Background (Bkgd)
Opening: ©Photodisc Green/Getty Images; Title Page: ©Goddard Space Flight Center/NASA; 2 ©Roger Tidman/Corbis; 4 ©SOHO (ESA & NASA)/NASA; 10 ©John M. Roberts/Corbis; 11 ©Taxi/ Getty Images; 12 ©James Randklev-Visions of America/Corbis; 13 ©Royalty-Free/Corbis; 16 ©Roger Ressmeyer/Corbis; 17 ©Jerry Schad/Photo Researchers, Inc.; 18 (B) NASA Image Exchange, (TC) ©Stone/Getty Images; 20 ©John Sanford/Photo Researchers, Inc.

ISBN: 0-328-13802-9

Earth and Space

by Harriet Stansbury

Glossary

axis an imaginary line through the center of Earth

constellation a group of stars that form a picture

crater a hole in the ground that is shaped like a bowl

orbit a path around another object

phase the shape of thwe lighted part of the Moon

rotation the spinning on an axis

solar system the planets and their moons and other objects that move around the Sun

What is the Sun?

You can see stars in the night sky.
Stars are made up of hot gases.
The Sun is a star.
You might think the Sun is the biggest star.
This is because the Sun is the closest star
to Earth.

The Sun is the center of the solar system.
Nine planets orbit the Sun.

Look at the picture.
Can you find Earth?

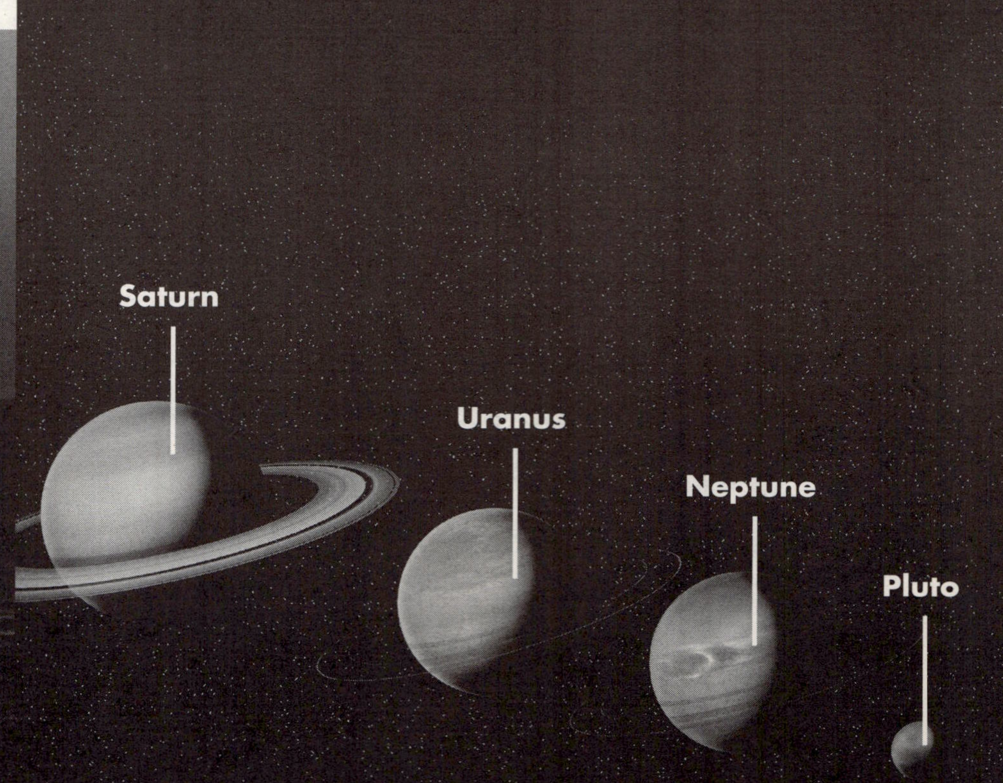

What is the solar system?

Earth is a planet.
Earth moves around the Sun.
Other planets move around the Sun.
The Sun, the Moon, Earth, other planets, and
their moons all make up the **solar system.**

The Sun is very bright.
This is why you cannot see other stars in
the day.

Why We Need the Sun

The Sun is far from us.
This makes it look small.
The Sun is really much bigger than Earth.

This is the Sun in space.

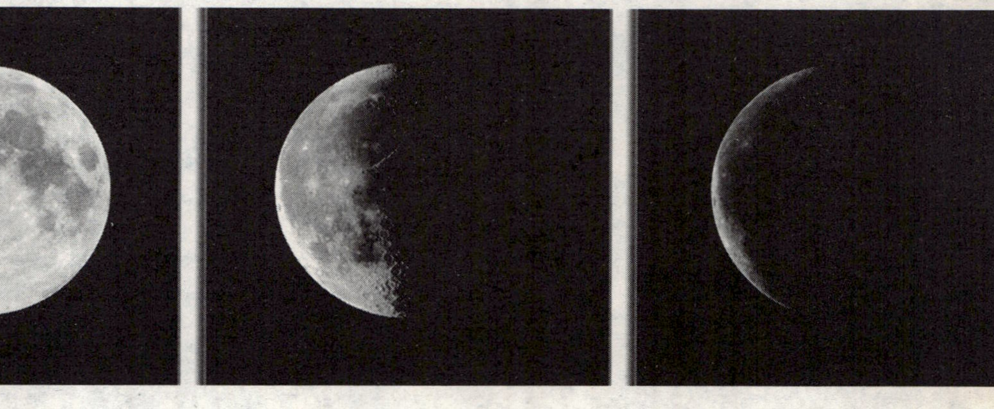

The shape of the Moon seems to change.
It may look round.
It may look like half of a circle.
At times you cannot see the Moon.
The shape of the lighted part of the Moon is
called a **phase.**

Why does the Moon change?

The Moon moves in an orbit around Earth.
The Moon orbits Earth while Earth orbits
the Sun.
It takes four weeks for the Moon to go
around Earth.

The Sun shines light on the Moon.
You can only see the part of the Moon that
is lit up.

We need the Sun.
Plants and animals need the Sun too.
The Sun gives living things light and heat.

What causes day and night?

Look at the picture.
You can see an imaginary line
through Earth.
This line is called an **axis.**
Earth spins on its axis.

You may see the Moon during the day.

Spinning on an axis is called a **rotation.**
Earth makes one full rotation each day.

The Moon

You can see the Moon at night.
The Moon is big and bright.

The Moon has hills and craters.
A **crater** is a hole.
A crater is shaped like a bowl.
Big rocks from space hit the Moon and
made craters.

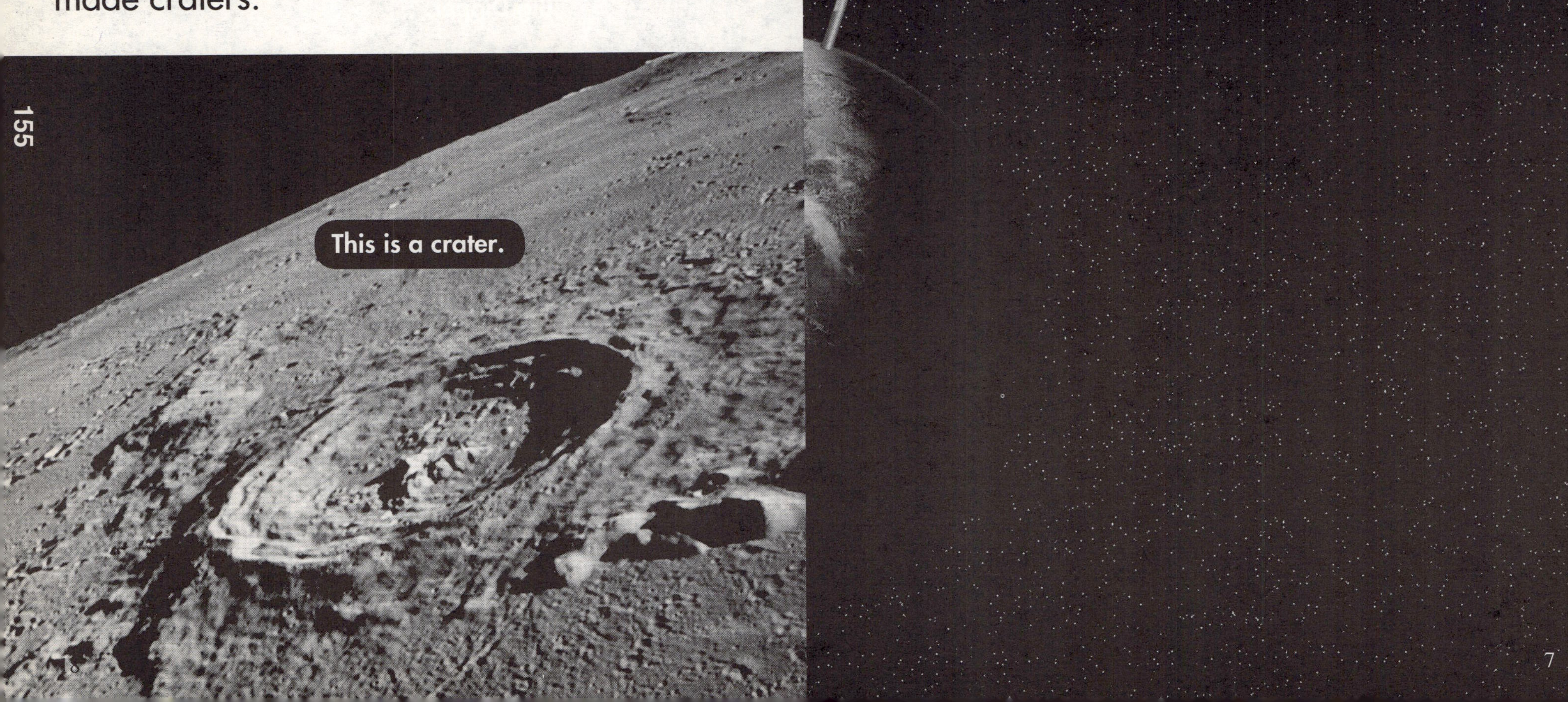

Earth's rotation makes day and night.
It is day when your side of Earth is facing
the Sun.

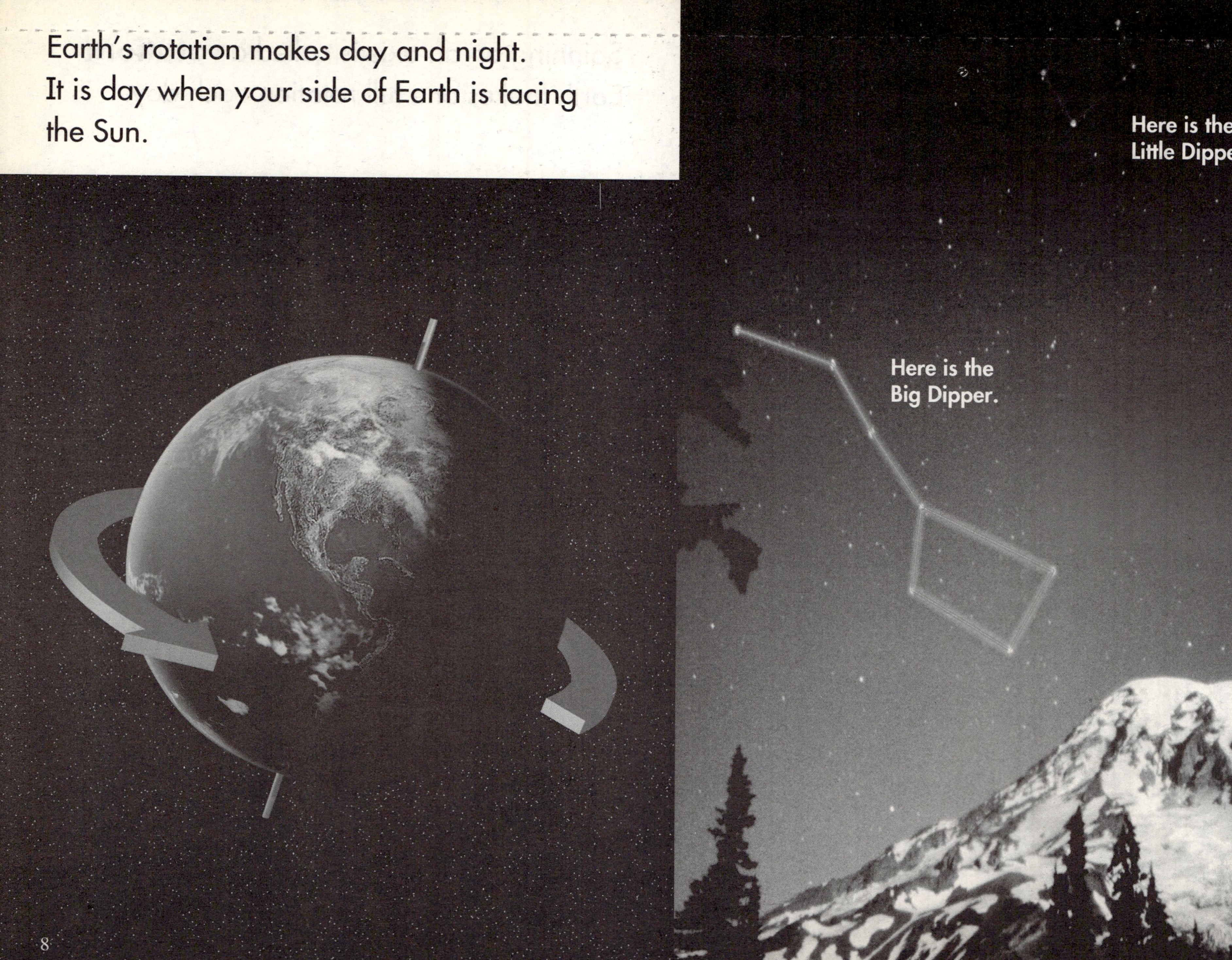

What can you see in the night sky?

You can see stars in the night sky.
The stars look small.
Stars are far from us.

People see pictures when they look
at the stars.
A group of stars that look like a picture
is called a **constellation.**

This constellation
looks like a lion.
It is called Leo.

It is night when your side of Earth is facing
away from the Sun.

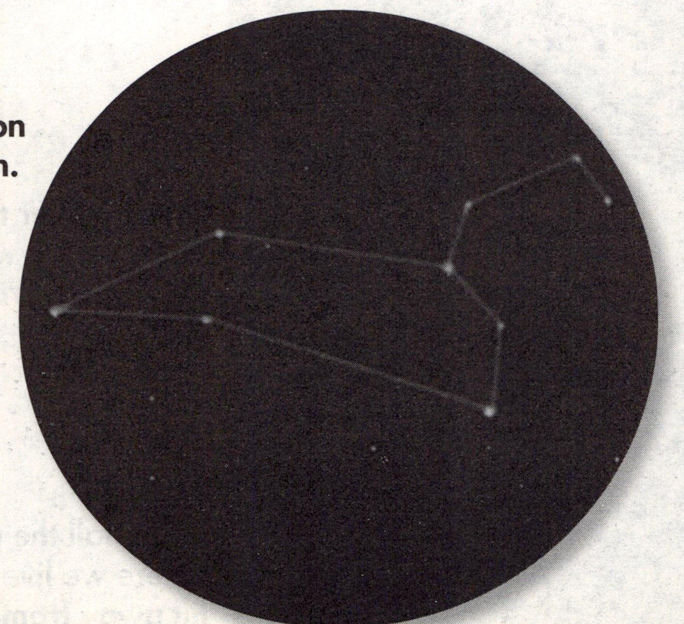

It takes 24 hours
for Earth to rotate
one time.

The Sun in the Sky

The Sun seems to go up and down in
the sky.
The Sun looks low in the sky in the morning.

Sunrise

It takes a year for Earth to move around
the Sun one time.
The tilt of Earth and Earth's orbit around
the Sun make the seasons change.

In the spring the part of Earth where
we live is starting to tilt toward the Sun.

In the winter the part of
Earth where we live is
titled away from the Sun.

In the fall the part of Earth
where we live is starting to
tilt away from the Sun.

What causes seasons to change?

Earth spins on its axis.
Earth is tilted on its axis.
Earth also makes an **orbit** around the Sun.
This means it moves in a path around
the Sun.

In the summer the part
of Earth where we live
is tilted toward the Sun.

At night, the Sun is low in the sky again.
The Sun is not moving.
It is Earth that is moving.

The Sun is always shining, but you cannot always see it.

Sunset

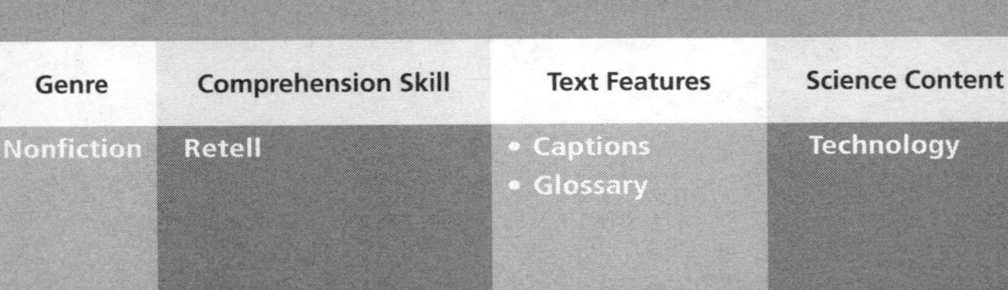

Technology
in Our World

by Arlene Block

Genre	Comprehension Skill	Text Features	Science Content
Nonfiction	Retell	• Captions • Glossary	Technology

Scott Foresman Science 2.13

PEARSON

Scott Foresman

DK

scottforesman.com

ISBN 0-328-13805-3

90000

9 780328 138050

Vocabulary

engine

invent

manufacture

meteorologist

satellite

technology

transportation

vaccine

What did you learn?

1. What are some ways people use technology?

2. What is a vaccine?

3. **Writing** in Science Technology helps meteorologists do their job. Write to tell how meteorologists use technology. Use words from the book as you write.

4. **Retell** Read pages 14–15. In your own words tell what it means to manufacture something.

Photographs: Every effort has been made to secure permission and provide appropriate credit for photographic material. The publisher deeply regrets any omission and pledges to correct errors called to its attention in subsequent editions. Unless otherwise acknowledged, all photographs are the property of Scott Foresman, a division of Pearson Education. Photo locators denoted as follows: Top (T), Center (C), Bottom (B), Left (L), Right (R) Background (Bkgd)
Opener: (Inset) ©Reuters NewMedia Inc./Corbis, (TC) ©Stone/Getty Images; Title Page: ©DK Images; 2 Getty Images; 3 ©Reuters/Corbis; 4 (C) ©David Mace/Robert Harding Picture Library Ltd., 4 (B) ©Reuters/Corbis; 5 (C) ©Taxi/Getty Images, (B) ©Giulio Andreini; 6 (BL) ©Steve Raymer/Corbis, (R) ©Bob Daemmrich/The Image Works, Inc., (BC) Hemera Technologies; 8 ©Taxi/Getty Images; 9 (TR) ©Taxi/Getty Images, (T) ©Lester Lefkowitz/Corbis; 10 (BR) ©Science Museum/Science & Society Picture Library, (BL) Getty Images; 11 (TL) Getty Images, (TR) Unisys Corporation; 12 ©DK Images; 13 (BL) ©David Young-Wolff/PhotoEdit, (CR) ©David Ducros/Photo Researchers, Inc., (B) ©Bob Daemmrich/StockBoston; 14 ©DK Images; 15 ©DK Images

ISBN: 0-328-13805-3

Technology in Our World

by Arlene Block

Glossary

engine a machine that makes something move or do work

invent to make something for the first time

manufacture to make by hand or by machine

meteorologist someone who studies weather

satellite an object that goes around another object

technology using science to solve problems

transportation the way people or things move from place to place

vaccine a medicine that can keep people from getting sick

What is technology?

Technology means using science to
solve problems.
People use computers.
People ride in cars.
We can do these things because
of technology.

Some materials are made by people.
A bicycle seat is made from plastic.
People make plastic.

Some materials come from nature.
This coat is made from wool.
Wool comes from sheep.

How do people make things?

People manufacture things we use.
Manufacture means to make by hand
or machine.
People use different materials to manufacture
different things.

14

People use technology to invent things.
Invent means to make something new.

People invent things we need.
We need cars and airplanes to travel.
People invent things we want.
Computer games are things we want.

3

Changes in Transportation

People and things move from place to place.
This is called **transportation.**

Technology helps with transportation.
It helps us travel fast and far.

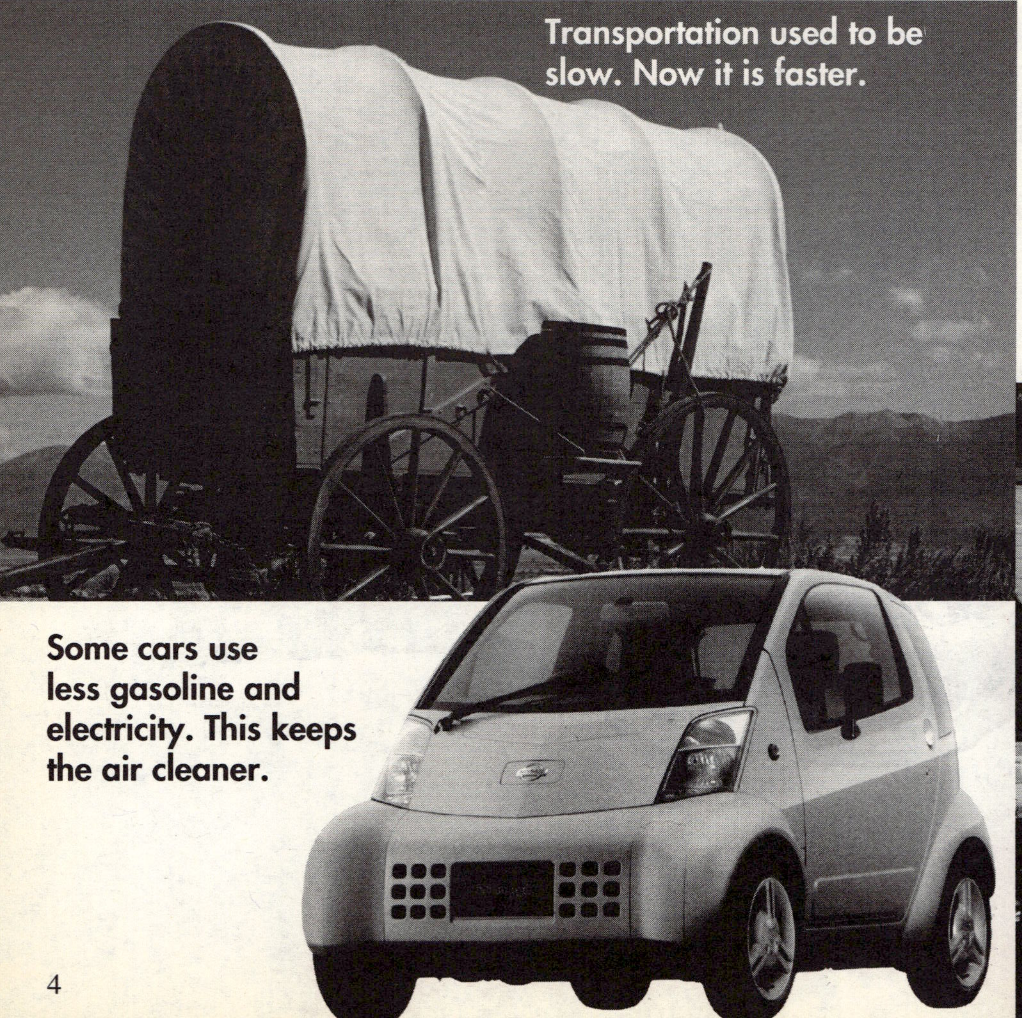

Some cars use less gasoline and electricity. This keeps the air cleaner.

A **meteorologist** studies weather.
Meteorologists get information from satellites.
A **satellite** is an object that moves around another object.
Pictures from satellites help meteorologists tell about the weather.

What are some other ways we use technology?

People can have fun using technology.
People listen to music or play games on computers.
People do work using technology.

An **engine** is a machine that does work or makes something move.
Steam engines were used for transportation long ago.
Now engines use gasoline or electricity to move trains, cars, boats, and planes.

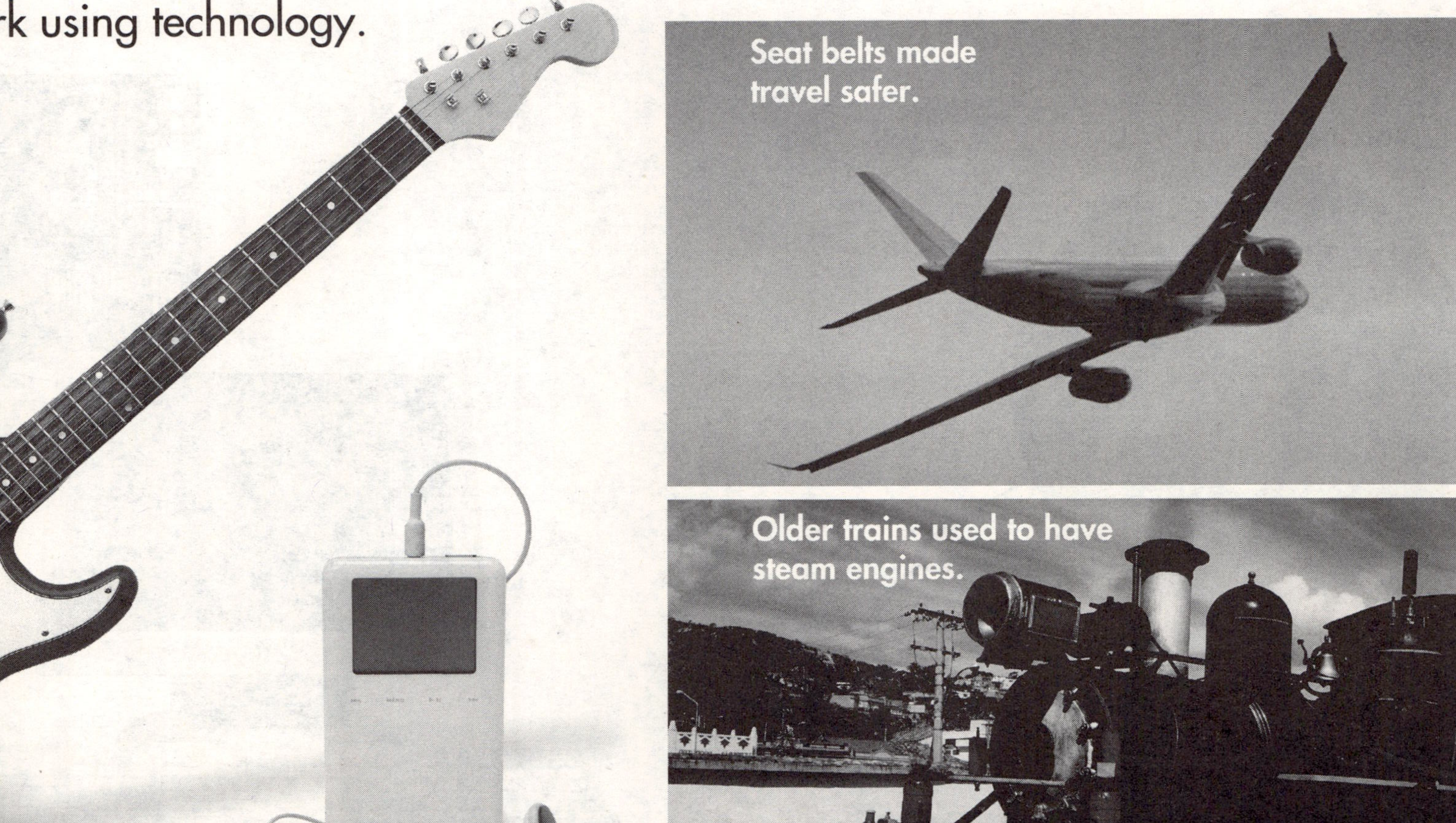

Seat belts made travel safer.

Older trains used to have steam engines.

How does technology help us?

Doctors use technology to help people.
A **vaccine** is a medicine.
Vaccines can keep us from getting sick.

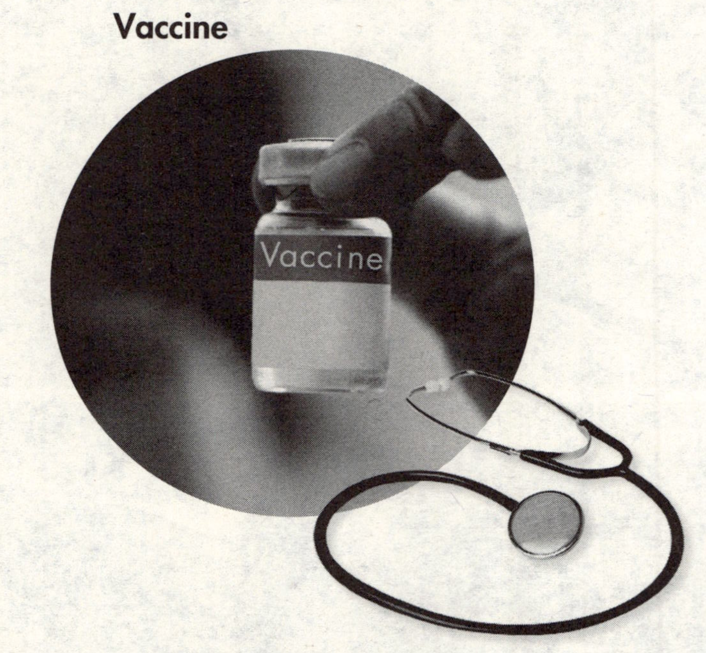
Vaccine

Some people communicate by computer.
The first computer was very big.
It filled a whole room!
Today computers are smaller and faster.
Technology can even help astronauts in space communicate with people on Earth.

How do we use technology to communicate?

Technology has changed how we communicate.
Some people communicate by telephone.
The first telephones stayed on a wall.
Today we can carry telephones with us.

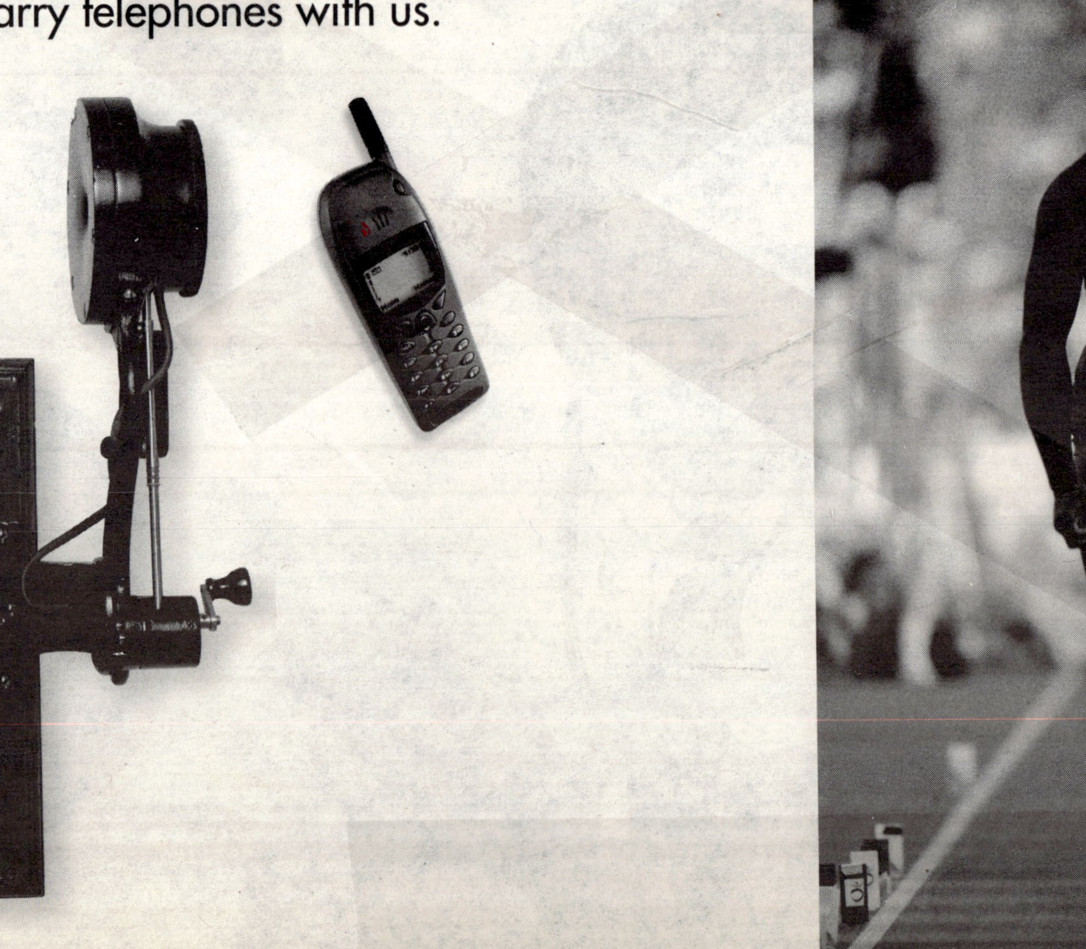

Glasses and hearing aids can be made because of technology.
Glasses help people see.
Hearing aids help people hear.

Technology helped people make this man's leg.

Doctors can see inside people with
special tools.
The tools help doctors learn why people
are sick.
Then doctors can help people get well.

Some tools are X rays, CAT scans,
and MRIs.
These tools were invented because
of technology.

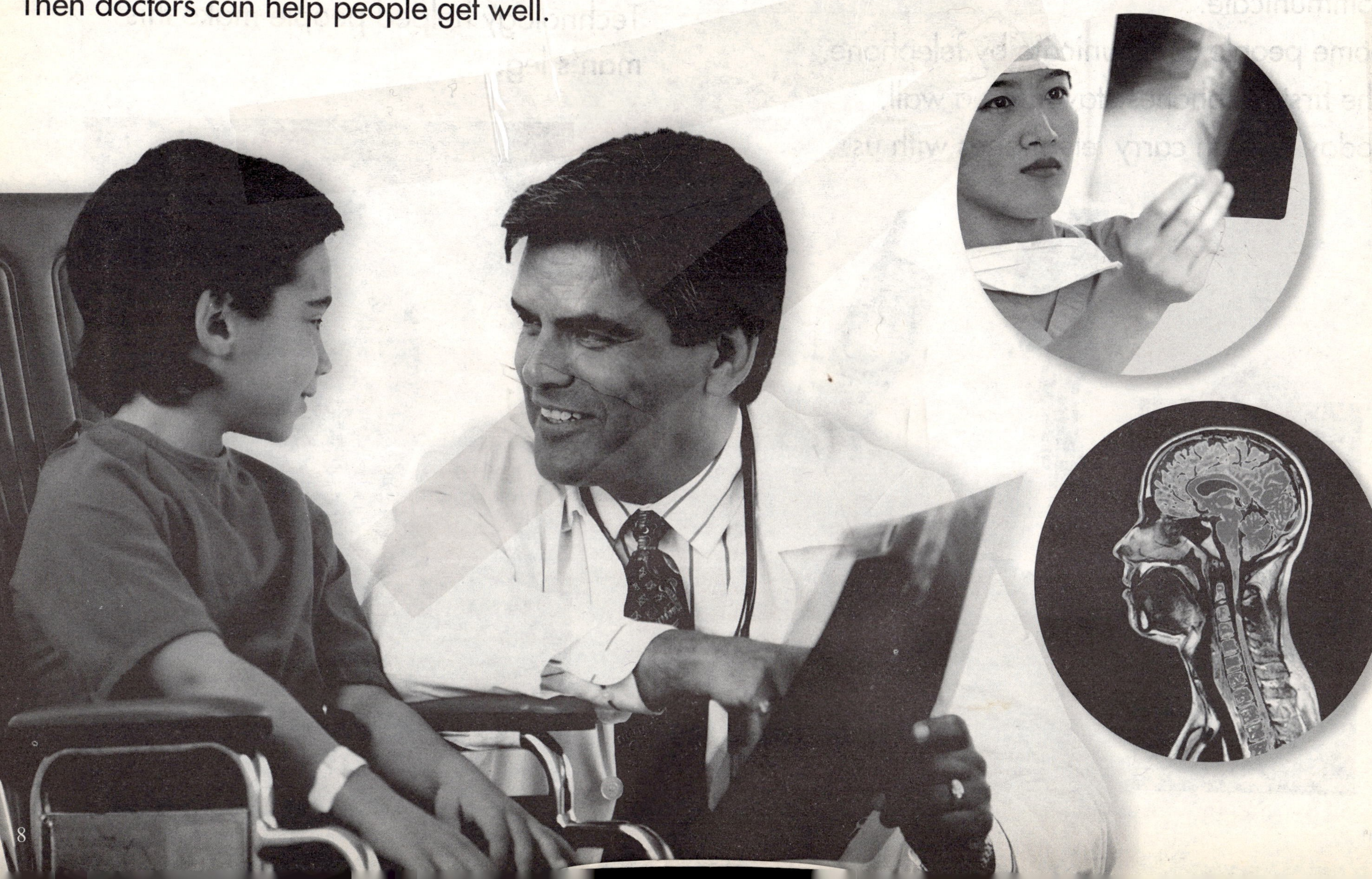